JOHN DOS PASSOS

Modern Literature Monographs

JOHN DOS PASSOS

George J. Becker

Frederick Ungar Publishing Co.
New York

Copyright © 1974 by Frederick Ungar Publishing Co., Inc.
Printed in the United States of America
Library of Congress Catalog Card Number: 74-78437
Designed by Anita Duncan
ISBN: 0-8044-2034-5

Contents

Chronology

1896:   John Dos Passos is born January 14, the son of John Randolph Dos Passos and Lucy Addison Sprigg Madison.

1907:   He enters Choate School, Wallingford, Conn.

1912–16:   He is a student at Harvard.

1917–18:   He is a member of the Norton-Harjes volunteer ambulance service in France and of the American Red Cross ambulance unit in Italy.

1918:   He enlists in the U.S. Army Medical Corps, serving in Europe from November until the following July.

1921:   *Three Soldiers* receives critical acclaim upon publication. Dos Passos makes a hazardous trip to the Caucasus and through the Middle East.

1924:   A meeting with Hemingway in Paris is the beginning of a close association lasting for more than ten years.

1925:   *Manhattan Transfer* is published.

1926–29:   He is a director of the New Playwrights' Theatre in New York.

1927:   He becomes involved in the attempt to save Sacco and Vanzetti, demonstrates in Boston, and writes "An Open Letter to President Lowell."

1928:   He spends several months in Russia.

1929:   He marries Katharine Smith.

1931:   Along with Dreiser and others he makes an investigative trip to the Harlan County, Kentucky mining region.

1934:   He signs "Open Letter to the Communist Party" in protest against its tactics in stifling dissent.

1937:   He makes a trip to Spain in aid of the Spanish Republic, is shocked by the extent of communist influence, and breaks with Hemingway.

1938:   The three novels of *U.S.A.* are published as a single volume.

1939:   The radical establishment turns against him for publication of *Adventures of a Young Man*.

1942–45:   He travels through the U.S., to the Pacific theater of war, and to Europe immediately after the war as a reporter.

1944:   He recovers paternal property in Westmoreland County, Virginia, and begins to renovate it as his permanent residence.

1947:   Katharine Dos Passos is killed in an automobile accident; Dos Passos loses the sight of one eye. He is elected to the American Academy of Arts and Letters.

1949:   He marries Elizabeth Holdridge.

1950:   Lucy Hamlin Dos Passos is born.

1957:   He receives the Gold Medal for Fiction from the National Institute of Arts and Letters.

1961:   Publication of *Midcentury* briefly stirs critical interest.

1967:   He receives the Feltrinelli Prize for fiction awarded by the Accademia dei Lincei in Rome.

1969:   He is present at Cape Canaveral for the Apollo 10 moonshot.

1970:   He dies of heart failure in Baltimore on September 28.

A Child of the Century

The role of artist-observer that John Dos Passos was destined to play was nurtured by the nature of the times in which he lived and by the unique circumstances of his life. Born in 1896, therefore reaching maturity during World War I, he, like others of his generation, came on stage at a turning point in the history of his country and of the entire western world. His preparation as a writer may be seen as four separate rites of passage, subjection to major ordeals of mind and spirit, which determined and tempered his view of the world and therefore the nature of his art.

He had, first 'of all, to come to grips with the actualities of life in the United States, from which he was isolated by the unusual circumstances of his birth and upbringing. Beyond that, World War I was to him a genuine initiation, a quick—and safe—plunge into the stream of real life that expunged the conventional expectations and beliefs of sheltered youth. The war also brought to a head the forces of socialism-communism, largely theoretical up to that point, in revolutions which were to provide a major cultural and intellectual referent for at least a generation. Siren song, intellectual pitfall, liberating vision, whatever the Russian experiment was, it had to be faced. Statesmen, artists, thinkers, above all historians of the twentieth century had to come to terms with that shattering phenomenon. Finally, for the aspiring writer there was the new milieu of the arts, somewhat belated in the United States, but when it did come as important for the development of the American writer as the ferment of the nineteenth century had been for his European counterpart.

In addition to these four major involvements there were two particular predilections of John Dos

Passos that helped to direct his thought and to determine the way he would synthesize his experience. He was from an early age an indefatigable traveler and was avid to report what he saw. And, controlling his observation of social structures and events was a political-philosophical bias that may most simply be identified as Jeffersonian. Without stretching truth too far, we may see in Dos Passos a man with the simplistic vision of the Enlightenment let loose in the dynamic chaos of the twentieth century. There is bound to be difference of opinion as to the accuracy of his judgment of that world, but there can be no doubt that in viewing and reporting it he was consistently his own man.

Except for the circumstances of his birth and childhood, his life was relatively uneventful, even colorless. There are no myths, no legends about John Dos Passos as there are about his contemporaries Ernest Hemingway and Scott Fitzgerald. He was not the darling of literary coteries (except briefly in the Thirties); he rarely went on the university lecture circuit; his name did not appear in fourteen-point type across the pages of *Life* and *Time*. Though he continued to write up to the time of his death in the fall of 1970, he was very much a private citizen, withdrawn to his farm in Westmoreland County, Virginia, cultivating his garden, reverting, almost, to his eighteenth-century persona, repudiating, perhaps, a world he never made, but mostly, one would think, taking on the philosophical detachment of age, which is less repudiation than recognition that there is little to do about the folly of mankind. For the better part of his life he magnificently presented both his hopes and his dissent. His hopes seemed overborne by events. His dissent, of the old-fashioned liberal stamp, seemed increasingly anachronistic. Thus when he died at the age of seventy-four, there was only brief, though respectful, notice. He already belonged to another age.

In *Chosen Country*, a late novel, which is a kind of autobiographical extrapolation, Dos Passos' double Jay Pignatelli wonders whether it is his myopia or his illegitimacy that has set him apart from his fellows. Yoking together these factors of grossly unequal weight suggests that the author did not suffer greatly from the irregularity of his birth. His one overtly auto-biographical work, *The Best Times* (1966), gives the facts of his illegitimacy without emotional coloring. His father was fifty-two when the son was born. Both parents had sons eighteen years older than he by their first unions. Since they could not legally marry until 1912 (after the death of the elder Dos Passos' first wife), the couple could live openly together only in Europe, where most of the boy's early childhood was spent. In his autobiography he recalls being taken to see a model of the Trans-Siberian Railroad at the Paris Exposition, accompanying his parents on a picnic in the English countryside with a man who looked like King Edward, seeing his father at a London hotel in court costume ready to be presented to the King and Queen, or, later in the United States, dining at Del-monico's and finding the meal and adult conversation unbearably tedious. The first "Camera Eye" in *U.S.A.* is a poignant evocation of a childhood fright at being caught up in a tumult of angry abuse by people in a foreign city who think that he and his mother are En-glish—this was at the time of the Boer War when the two were living in Brussels.

There is a casual comment in *The Best Times* that

he "never had a proper family life and was developing an unexpressed yearning for it," in reference to his enjoyment of being with the Gerald Murphy family in France during the 1920s. What we must infer is less a sense of being set apart by his illegitimacy—he comments on one occasion that he thought it rather romantic—than a kind of emotional feast or famine condition in which he and his mother lived in seclusion and quiet for long periods until the arrival of the glamorous and exuberant father suddenly gave life a kind of fairytale enchantment. The small boy had no home, no routine, no companions, and most of the time no father. There was the further indignity of having to attend an English school, where by name, appearance, and background he was utterly alien. He hated the experience and by 1910 had won his battle to be educated in the United States, where he was enrolled at Choate.

Though his contact with his father was limited, there is evidence of strong influence. The older man was an embodiment of the American dream. Son of an immigrant from Punta do Sol on the island of Madeira, he "cherished the dream of the perfect republic based on the Anglo-Saxon tradition of individual liberty with justice for rich and poor." He was an ardent abolitionist, ran off to the Civil War as a youngster, and served as a drummer in a Pennsylvania regiment. After the war he studied law and in 1867 hung up his shingle in New York City. His rise to fame and fortune was phenomenal even for those times. He soon specialized in stock brokerage cases and in the field of corporate organization, working out the reorganization of the Erie and other railroads and writing books on the subject. Money flowed in, but he was very much the con-

spicuous spender of the Gilded Age. In his son's time
he owned a 100-foot steam yacht, which plied up and
down the Potomac. Only in the years after his wife's
death did he take thought for the future, too late to
leave the young man much in the way of an inheri-
tance, not that the latter ever complained about his
change of fortune.

In his eighteenth-century way the father tried to
form his son's mind, directing his reading, pressing
books into his hands each time he saw him, encouraging the youngster to write to him in French, and im-
buing him with something of his own political philos-
ophy. One of the passions of the elder Dos Passos was
the Anglo-Saxon heritage of law, both common and
constitutional. He saw in this a basis for union among
all English-speaking peoples, in the book *The Anglo-
Saxon Century* advocating such a union as a means to
counter the power of Russia and to insure peace for
the century to come. He was a vigorously political
animal. In addition to his adherence to the abolitionist
cause in the Civil War, he was deeply moved by the
Cuban struggle for independence at the turn of the
century. In politics a lifelong Democrat, he favored
the conservative Cleveland against Bryan, though he
later came around to accepting McKinley. Initially he
could not abide Theodore Roosevelt and campaigned
for Alton B. Parker in 1904. (In his English school that
year the boy was joined by another American youngster, who promptly knocked him down when he
learned that young John was for Parker.) During the
campaign the father issued a pamphlet denouncing
the Republican Party for its reversal of Lincoln's policy
of conciliation, for packing the Supreme Court, for
cheating Tilden out of the presidency in 1876, for the

seizure of Panama, and for excessive centralization of government. He campaigned for Champ Clark in 1912 but supported Wilson in 1916. He was a man of conservative probity and passion, divorcing in some way his participation in the world of malefactors of great wealth from the political morality of that milieu.

John Dos Passos' addiction to travel was indirectly part of the paternal influence. Not only was he of necessity a rolling stone in his childhood years, but in 1911, when he had passed the Harvard exams at fifteen, his father sent him off on a typical eighteenth-century grand tour under the direction of "a young man named Jones, who had some classical attainments and was planning to become a Dominican monk." In 1916 upon graduation from Harvard he was deterred from joining an ambulance unit in France by his father's offer of a winter in Spain to perfect his Spanish and study architecture. In 1917, a few months after his father's death, he returned to Europe as "a gentleman volunteer," first with the Norton-Harjes ambulance unit, then with the American Red Cross, and finally in the medical corps of the American army. In the first two of these assignments travel seemed to be the be-all and the end-all of his existence. He and his companions had a remarkable capacity for ignoring and extending travel orders so as to go wherever they wanted. After the Armistice he managed to get himself attached to the Sorbonne detachment in Paris and spent several happy months before demobilization, when he promptly went off to Spain as correspondent for a British labor paper. A little later he joined the Near East Relief in Turkey and the Caucasus, from there making his way—in the fashion Richard Halliburton was to romanticize a few years later—to Iran

and then, by improbable means, through the still em-
battled desert to Beirut. There was little of the world
that he did not see during the next fifty years, Brazil
becoming a prime interest in the 1960s because of its
Portuguese origins. But it was to Europe that he returned as regularly as clockwork up until World War
II, usually defraying his expenses by writing magazine
articles. As he remarked about going steerage on the
Paris in 1925, "Locomotion even under the most ad-
verse conditions always cheers me up."

What these early biographical details add up to is
that Dos Passos was peculiarly cut off from the American scene of which he was to be the chief chronicler.
In significant respects he was denied the ordinary experiences of the youth of his time. He knew nothing of
the country except what he saw from the train between Washington and Boston. Choate and Harvard
were upper-class citadels. His favorite haunt at his father's estate on the Potomac in Virginia was anachronistic. The nearest he came to participation in "real
life" was in the summer of 1912 when, with his father
politicking in Baltimore, he had to run the house, pay
the bills, fire the drunken maid, and clean up the
vomit she left behind her. It is no wonder then that
when he finished Harvard and was a free man after his
father's death, he was avid for experience. He was
fortunate in his time. As one critic puts it, "Like other
Harvard aesthetes, Dos Passos was suddenly overtaken
by history."

History for him and his contemporaries was the
twisted strand of events issuing from World War I:
the war itself, the Russian Revolution, the Versailles
settlement, the socialist-communist movement in its
many manifestations in many places, the depression,

and World War II—some thirty years of agitated involvement in experiences that had to be assimilated and evaluated if one was to survive. Young Dos Passos and his contemporaries were emotionally and philosophically unprepared to cope with these experiences; they had to find their way through the dark wood of the new world, where long-standing landmarks had been obliterated, by trial and error. Some achieved this by grouping together in a pack; others, like Dos Passos, made it alone.

Leaving out of account the ephemeral appeal of slogans like "Make the World Safe for Democracy," World War I had a romantic attraction for an American youth in 1916. Far from the actuality of conflict, he could think of war in terms of heroic deeds, providing a stage on which he might act out the role of a latterday Bayard—"sans peur et sans reproche." Fear was the actuality he would speedily discover, and "reproche," the stains on character, would be seen to be such venal things as scrounging for advantage, for a bottle of wine, a girl, a higher rank, a medal. This was the pattern for men at war, not heroism. Nonetheless, the war was a breaking out from limitation, moral and physical, from the boredom and restrictions of the small town and the farm. It brought exposure to a different culture; it brought release from inhibition. In the words of the popular war song, "How are you going to keep them down on the farm after they've seen Paree?" In short, the war changed men's lives, Dos Passos' life no less than the lives of others. He went off to war three times, first as tourist in the fall of 1916, sailing up the Gironde to Bordeaux, the safe capital of wartime France; then in the next year as a member of the ambulance corps to Bordeaux, Paris, and the front near Verdun; and finally as an enlisted man in the Army Medical Corps. From the number of times he portrayed the experience of war in his novels, we can judge that it was a turning point in his life, an initiation into life, as the title of his first published novel indicates.

The most anguished experience of Dos Passos' life was his hot-cold involvement with socialism and communism. In this too he was very much a man of his time, though always with his characteristic independent stance. The blandishments of socialism had long been in the air—witness the conversion of Upton Sinclair by the time he wrote *The Jungle* in 1906—but it was the Russian Revolution that gave them focus and force. The war was a powerful lesson in the folly and injustice, not to mention criminality, of the current society. The revolution came pat as an apparently viable alternative. Lincoln Steffens' famous judgment, "I have seen the future, and it works," was what all young men of goodwill wanted and needed to believe. This need was continued and intensified in the period of postwar readjustment and depression. Yet faith in the future heralded by the Russian experiment had at some point to meet the test of how it worked. For some disillusionment came very late. For Dos Passos it came early. His contemporaries on the left wanted to believe that he was one of them. When they found out that he was not, they turned on him in vituperative abuse, dimming, if not destroying, his literary reputation for the rest of his life.

It is important to note that Dos Passos was never a man of doctrine, never a hard-line adherent of party. His was the young liberal's openness, an initially uncritical eagerness to believe, but never a permanent suspension of critical judgment. Before going to Europe in 1917 he attended radical meetings on New York's East Side among the Jewish socialists, read *The Masses*, protested the declaration of war and conscription, and with juvenile enthusiasm declared, "I am thinking of becoming a revolutionist!" Years later in more sober mood he said of himself at that time: "Suddenly I believed I was a socialist. Even then I think I marveled a little at the suddenness with which passionate convictions develop in the youthful mind. In the spring of 1917 some people caught socialism the way others caught the flu." But at that time his social views and his feelings about the war were inextricably intertwined. Increasingly he felt that "The secret aim of American intervention was to quench the European revolution." Therefore, to be a pacifist was to protest against both the war and the whole miserable social mess.

The repressive measures instigated at home by Attorney General A. Mitchell Palmer gave substance to this belief. "Hate the Hun" was swiftly followed by "Hate the Reds," whether they were to be identified as socialists, communists, anarchists, or I.W.W.s (International Workers of the World, colloquially known as Wobblies). Since there was coercion, repression, annihilation of dissidence on all sides, it was a writer's self-evident duty to combat them, to lend his pen and his person to liberal causes. The immediate obligation was to support *The New Masses* (*The Masses* had been suppressed during the hysteria of the war), which, Dos Passos said, "was organized in an effort to build a pulpit for native American radicalism. We felt that the Marxist Leninist line did not apply to the United States." Granting his lack of interest in organizations

as such, he felt his socialist affiliations were justified as
a means of getting to know the labor movement. His
colleagues were never easy about him: "The hardcore
dogmatists were already leery of my attitude. Though
I hadn't yet read Roger Williams I was already the
Seeker in matters political as he was the Seeker in
matters religious."

It was by doing an article for *The New Masses*
that he got involved in the Sacco-Vanzetti case, which
became the prime focus of liberal indignation in the
mid-Twenties. Later he accepted an assignment by the
communist *Daily Worker* to report the agitation in
behalf of the anarchists Sacco and Vanzetti in Boston
during the summer of 1927: "Though I was thoroughly
aware of the tension between the Communists and the
anarchist defense committee, my attitude, somewhat
naive at the time, was that it didn't matter where you
published so long as they printed what you wrote."
While in Boston he went on a picket line along with
Lillian Hellman, Dorothy Parker, Edna St. Vincent
Millay and others, and got picked up by the police.
Months later he stood trial and was acquitted. He was
the author of an open letter to President Lowell of
Harvard, which appeared in *The Nation*. This, like all
efforts in support of the condemned men, was unavailing; the two men were executed on August 23, 1927,
crystallizing for the moment Dos Passos' feelings that
the whole sorry scheme of things would have to be
restructured by radical action.

Looking back on this period almost forty years
later in *The Best Times*, the author pointed to "the
violence of the revulsion against foreigners and radicals that went through the United States after the first
world war" as embodying "the evil passions that mili-

tarism fed on." To the young of that generation, support of Sacco and Vanzetti was a necessary gesture in defense of freedom of speech and justice. But the experience carried another lesson. The protest, initially spontaneous, was taken over by the Communist Party for its own purposes; it had learned that "Griefs and discontents, properly stimulated and directed, were more effective than armies in the world struggle for power." Dos Passos felt that he had been used:

This sort of controversy wasn't in my line. For one thing I could never convince myself enough of the rightness of my own opinions properly to take out after my opponents. I could never quite get used to people I thought were friends getting sore at me personally instead of at my reprehensible opinions. [These] ideological rumbles around the Sacco-Vanzetti case and the New Playwrights' Theatre got my head to spinning so I decided to pull out of New York for a while. I craved fresh air and I had to have some sleep.

Affiliation with the leftwing theater, an almost traumatic experience, coincided with involvement in the Sacco-Vanzetti case. Coming home in 1926, he says he was suddenly convinced that it was his business to report the rebellions of the men he had known in the army. Thus he accepted an invitation to be a director of John Howard Lawson's New Playwrights' Theatre. There for a time he was committed to a program and had to subordinate his own aesthetic gropings to the doctrinaire approach of a group. For the better part of three years he gave himself to this enterprise. At the end he withdrew in disgust at the straitjacket of an aesthetic that was not his own and, as it happened, an ideological control that he found repugnant.

The men who founded the New Playwrights' Theatre (Lawson, Michael Gold, and others) induced Otto Kahn, the financier, to put up money to support their experimental group; they were to provide the plays and the direction. They looked upon the Russian revolutionary theater with envy, seeing that regime as a laboratory for both social organization and the arts. As early as 1923, Dos Passos, in a preface he wrote for Lawson's play *Roger Bloomer*, delivered himself in similar vein:

The continuously increasing pressure in the grinding engine of industrial life will force other safety valves than baseball and the movies and the Ku Klux Klan. Something approximating a national theatre is the most direct organ of group consciousness and will come into being, inevitable with the welding of our cities into living organisms out of the junk heaps of boxed and predatory individuals that they are at present.

This tortured prose is an attempt to express a confused conviction of vague but hopeful intent, an intent that vacillates between the aesthetic and the political. "Toward a Revolutionary Theatre," a statement he wrote for *The New Masses* in 1927, is more explicit:

By revolutionary I mean that such a theatre must break with the present theatrical tradition, not with the general traditions of the theatre, and that it must draw its life and ideas from the conscious actions of the industrial and white-collar working classes which are out to get control of the great flabby mass of capitalist society and mold it to their own purpose.

The manifesto of the group at large declared their intention to produce only American plays, with active management in the hands of the five "working play-wrights." They intended to provide a theater that would serve the new author and would be a "clearing house for ideas and a focus for social protest." Though Dos Passos did provide three plays, it turned out that his chief activity was stage design and his chief interest the aesthetic possibilities of the movement.

With the onset of the depression and the ensuing tensions in international politics, Dos Passos remained concerned but increasingly uncommitted to party or program. He went with Theodore Dreiser and others to investigate conditions among the coal miners in Harlan County, Kentucky, in the fall of 1931, edited the volume *Harlan Miners Speak*, and was arrested for criminal syndicalism. The Communist Party leaders wanted him to stand trial, in that way publicizing their efforts in behalf of the miners. He felt he had more important things to do than go to prison and refused to become a martyr for the Party's cause. His final venture into activism was a project, in which Lillian Hellman, Ernest Hemingway, and Archibald MacLeish participated, to make a movie about the Spanish Civil War on behalf of the Madrid government. After a few months of observation and bureaucratic frustration, he broke with Hemingway because he was unwilling to sacrifice truth to propaganda and because he saw the Spanish cause becoming increasingly a pawn to Stalinist power politics. Once more he was convinced that the Communist Party used people and events for its own ends without regard for liberal principle, an opinion that was embodied in his next novel, *Adventures of a Young Man*. From that time on he was regularly assailed by the orthodox left, and his reputation as writer and as liberal was left in tatters by a fusillade of criticism from doctrinaire critics who a few months before had mistakenly hailed him as a leading apologist of the socialist-communist cause.

Less dramatic, but ultimately more important for his art, were the new winds of literary doctrine and taste which caught Dos Passos up in his formative years. The development from Harvard aesthete to individual and original writer of fiction was very much conditioned by time and place. Experience came at the right time. The lessons he had learned from his reading came to the surface as he needed them. He was also the associate of other writers who felt the same impulsion as hè to break through convention and to create something new and relevant to their times. For more than fifty years European literature had been dominated by the realists and naturalists, writers convinced that the here and now was as valuable for literary expression as the hackneyed stories drawn from classic sources and medieval romance, and that the plight of the common man and woman was as poignant as the tribulations of knights on horseback and asexual fainting maidens. The object of this crusade was truth, not beauty, though Flaubert, the pioneer French realist, maintained that beauty could be achieved out of commonplace materials. It was important to show the conditions of human existence as they really were, to strip the veils of illusion from pious sentiment and concealed exploitation. To reach these ends, it was also necessary to develop a new style, one that was matter-of-fact, relatively unadorned, in short, documentary. French, Russian, Scandinavian, Spanish, and Italian writers had all distinguished themselves in this mode. Only in England and the United States was there reluctance to go all out in the depiction of things as they are.

Suddenly after the war the dam burst in the United States with the appearance of a whole new generation of experimenters and plain speakers. Sherwood Anderson, Sinclair Lewis, Ernest Hemingway, Scott Fitzgerald, E. E. Cummings (whom Dos Passos knew at Harvard and in France), even the older Dreiser, were Dos Passos' friends and acquaintances. We do not know how much the young author talked with these men and with them reflected on the new goals of the writer. He does tell us that he had read Flaubert for years and had caught the latter's "obsession for the *mot juste*." He had early become familiar with the great Russian novelists "in yellow-backed French editions." In Madrid during his post-graduation travels he met writers of the Generation of '98, those Spanish writers who forced a turn away from outmoded literary conventions to an examination of contemporary issues. Now he saw the possibility of doing what these foreigners had done in terms of his own environment and experience. And before him was the monumental example of Theodore Dreiser:

It was the ponderous battering ram of his novels that opened the way through the genteel reticences of American nineteenth-century fiction for what seemed to me to be a truthful depiction of people's lives. Without Dreiser's treading out a path for naturalism none of us would have had a chance to publish even.

As early as 1915, Dos Passos had sworn in a letter "by all the gods of Flaubert, of Homer, of modern realism and the new poetry," that "Prize fights are every bit as good a subject for poetry as fine ladies and illicit love affairs," and a few months later that "You can find a sort of mad splendor in things, the ugliest, the filthiest things, if you really look for it." At the time he wrote these sentiments he was merely echoing Flaubert and was not practicing what he preached. It took both the disillusioning experience of war and the energizing contact with his contemporaries to lead him out of the stuffy domain of literary convention.

Though never a member of the "lost generation," Dos Passos was sporadically a part of the transatlantic migration that populated the Left Bank of Paris during the 1920s. Two things set him apart: his aloofness from trends and coteries and his private love affair with France, which long preceded this period. Moreover, he had no desire to fight for a place in the pecking order of the expatriates. By reason of his early success with *Three Soldiers*, he was on a more than equal footing with Fitzgerald, Hemingway, and the others who made Paris their headquarters.

Dos Passos probably first met Hemingway during their ambulance corps days in Italy in 1918. They met again in Paris and had become intimate by 1924. One of the things that brought them together was their enthusiasm for things Spanish. Dos Passos was not present in Pamplona during the bull running immortalized in *The Sun Also Rises*, but he was there the next year with a whole crowd of what he called "fake bohemians." After the San Fermin celebrations he and others walked through the Pyrenees from Pamplona to Andorra. Another year he joined the Hemingways for skiing in Austria, and in the fall of 1930, very much out of character, he went elk hunting with Hemingway near Cooke, Montana. In *The Best Times* he speculates that it was he who discovered Key West and told Hem about it. In any case the two authors spent much time together in that as yet undeveloped resort, and it was there that Dos Passos met Katharine Smith, his future wife, who had grown up with the Hemingways. Some years after their marriage they were with Hem when he had the epic struggle with a tuna which was to provide the basis of *The Old Man and the Sea*. Eventually friendship abated as Hemingway became overbearing and the Dos Passos couple refused to kowtow to him. Hem resented their trying to keep him "kidded down to size." They found it was better to stay apart, but in 1933 when Dos Passos was suffering from a bout of the rheumatic fever that plagued him all his life, Hemingway generously sent $1000 to tide him over a bad period.

In much the same way, in spite of his involvement in the New Playwrights' Theatre, he was in Greenwich Village but not of it. As he observed retrospectively: "In the private universe I was arranging for myself, literary people generally, and particularly Greenwich Village and Paris exiles, were among the excommunicated categories. Their attitude toward life made me want to throw up. But as soon as I got to be friends with one of them he or she became the exception, unique and unassailable." Yet upon his return to the United States in 1922 he found himself very much part of that milieu. He roomed for a time in the same house as Hart Crane. Lunch with Scott and Zelda Fitzgerald in October 1922 was "the beginning of an epoch." Sherwood Anderson was there, and in the afternoon they all drove out to Great Neck, which was to be the setting of *The Great Gatsby*. Then they called on Ring Lardner. It was through Fitzgerald that he came to know John Peale Bishop and Edmund Wilson. Donald Ogden Stewart was part of the circle. Whittaker

Chambers, "then a spooky little guy on hush-hush missions as a Communist Party courier, flitted in and out." His friend Nagel was painting in Washington Square. Schofield Thayer and Sibley Watson, who had taken over *The Dial*, moved it from Chicago to New York. At this time he even went to meet Dreiser, who "had no small talk and neither did I."

The significant thing is that Dos Passos had the strength to escape literary coteries just as he escaped ideological coteries. He maintained his independence throughout his life. He was, as he put it in 1959, "a borderer, a dweller in no man's land." Purged of the first fine frenzy of revolutionary political ideas, he settled down to an undramatic reporting of his times. During the war he went on extended tours to both the European and the Pacific theaters. He attended the Nuremberg trials. His first marriage came to a cruel end in 1947, when his wife was killed in an automobile accident and he lost an eye. He remarried in 1949 and rejoiced in the birth of a daughter in 1950. Ten years earlier he had managed to retrieve part of his father's estate in Westmoreland County, Virginia, a heritage that had been withheld from him for a quarter of a century. He settled there permanently in 1946. By his residence in Tidewater Virginia and by his almost obsessive absorption in the life and times of Jefferson and other Founding Fathers, he increasingly withdrew from the arena of contemporary life which he had meticulously and caustically observed. He kept on traveling and he kept on writing to the extent that failing health would permit. At his death in September 1970 another novel, which he referred to as "The Thirteenth Chronicle," was virtually completed.

his contemporaries were completely disenchanted w
their country's role in the war, attacking "the swa
bellied old fogies in frock-coats" for the "goddamn
mess they've made of organized society, the banke
and brokers and meatpackers and business men! Be
ter any tyranny than theirs!" He and his literary com
panions talked together of going back home to "figh
with pen and tooth and nail for free speech and gen
eral liberty—to try to make a splash, however small, in
the stagnant puddle of the American mind." It was in
this ferment of emotion and rebellion that he tacitly
gave up the idea of dying on the barricades, judging
that "My business was to tell the tale." Looking back
fifty years later, he is depressed by "the greenhorn
enthusiasms" of his youth but willing to concede that
"What the young have that is unique is an unjaded
apparatus for registering experience; keen eyes, sharp
ears, eager senses."

Three Soldiers (1921) brought that capacity for
registering experience into play on a broader and more
comprehensive scale. It was timely, and its success was
immediate. There had never been a war novel like it.
To a large extent it set the pattern of realistic war
novels for the next thirty years, until relief from the
grimness of war was sought by demonstration of its
absurdity, as in *Catch 22*. Dos Passos had little in the
way of models to work from. Immediately before him
was Henri Barbusse's *Under Fire*, which he had enthusiastically read in French as soon as it came out,
but its lyrical and impressionistic manner was something that he sought to avoid. Obviously no American
novelist was likely to overlook Stephen Crane's *The
Red Badge of Courage*, which, contrived though it is,
conveys much of the actuality of war. But Dos Passos

2

∿∿

First Flights

Released from the war, at last his own man, Dos Passos spent the decade of the Twenties in artistic experiment. His Harvard years, however much he lambasted them, however much he deprecated himself as one of the "deadly serious young men" who edited *The Harvard Monthly*, contributed to *Eight Harvard Poets*, and considered their imitative, arty works "more important, somehow, than the massacres around Verdun," were not wasted. It was while in Harvard that he discovered a copy of *Blast* containing some of T. S. Eliot's early poems. It was there that his artistic horizons were expanded by the Diaghilev Ballet, new productions at the Boston opera, and the innovative painting shown in the United States for the first time at the famous Armory Show in 1912. He went to Spain in 1917 to study architecture. He became enamored of painting. In Paris after the war, he was exhilarated by the nonsense of the Dada movement, and he was soon spouting the doctrines of expressionism as it was embodied in the new German theater. He published volumes of poetry and of travel impressions. He wrote plays and designed stage sets. Even after the success of his novel *Three Soldiers*, he still thought that painting might be his proper vocation, and in 1923 he exhibited his work (along with paintings by Adelaide J. Lawson and sculpture by Ruben Nakian). He professed no commitment to the novel, giving the impression at thirty that he was still a dilettante, until suddenly he found himself immersed in the vast labor of the *U.S.A.* trilogy. His path was set.

When he reached the United States in the fall of 1920 he had the somewhat ambiguous distinction of being a published writer. His novel *One Man's Initiation—1917*, salvaged from a work projected by him

and Robert Hillyer while they were in the am corps together, was scribbled down on board sh returned home in 1918. Almost by chance it f the hands of a London publisher and, after son sorship and a monetary contribution by the au appeared in 1920. It sold sixty-eight copies months. A slight work, it bears much the same r to his later writings as Tolstoy's *Sevastopol* be *War and Peace*. In each case there is an evident to bear truthful witness to the facts of war w much in the way of technical expertise. Certainly Passos' work is not the great war novel that he sa was planning in his mind a few weeks after he ar in France with the ambulance corps (and befor had any real experience of war). Rather it is an ur tentious series of impressions held together by the periences of the fictional Martin Howe and his s kick Tom Randolph in their non-combatant role ambulance drivers. The novel is highly visual, m up of scores of vignettes of war. The narrative dict is unduly poetic, but the dialogue mostly rings tr and over all there is little arty straining for effect.

The author thought well enough of it to allow to be republished twice during his lifetime, though rightly leaves it (and *Streets of Night*) out of the li ing of his Contemporary Chronicles. In an introdu tion which he provided for the 1968 reissue of t work he tells of its emotional and ideological matri The more he saw of the war—much as he enjoyed th travel and adventure—the more futile and wasteful appeared to him. He became so indignant in his letter that the Italian censors began to take an interest i him, with the result that his contract with the Rec Cross was not renewed in the spring of 1918. He and

went further than either of these models, shifting the focus from men at war to war itself.

He did this in two ways: by means of a comprehensive metaphor and by means of a realistic cross section. The metaphor states bluntly that the army is a machine that dehumanizes men, that it is without mind and feeling and destroys mind and feeling in all whom it touches. The section headings convey this in logical progression: "Making the Mould," "The Metal Cools," "Machines," "Rust," "Under the Wheels." Then Section Five, "The World Outside," deserts the metaphor in order to remind the reader of another way of being. The metaphor is obvious—once someone thought of it—and the author makes the most of it, contrasting mechanical process with the rhetorical camouflage by which the machine is concealed and ennobled. Patriotism, making the world safe for democracy, punishing the Hun—myriad slogans to manipulate men's minds—all of these are meaningless and irrelevant when one looks at the inexorable grinding away of the machine.

The narrative in verification of this offers a threefold example of men in war, supported by numerous background figures. There is nothing new in this device: Tolstoy in *War and Peace* had done the same thing with Andrei Bolkonsky, Nikolai Rostov, and Pierre Bezukhov. The strategy of such a limited cross section demands that the three examples be from such broadly varied areas of experience that they give the impression of providing a complete induction and that no one of them have primacy as *the* protagonist. In this latter respect the novel goes astray: it does not achieve the evenhandedness which is the brilliant hallmark of Dos Passos' mature works.

The three representative figures are Dan Fuselli from San Francisco, an immigrant's son dominated by typical middle-class ambition to get ahead; Chrisfield, an Indiana farm boy, a primitive both in terms of his limited experience of life and in the violent immediacy of his emotions; and John Andrews, Virginia bred, Harvard educated, with a somewhat amorphous talent for music. At the end of the novel Fuselli has survived; Chrisfield, AWOL in Paris, is seeking escape and will probably make it, though he is constantly under the threat of having his murder of a sergeant discovered; and Andrews, who has escaped from a labor battalion to which he has been assigned as punishment for breaking the rules, is picked up by the Military Police and faces twenty years in federal prison. None of the men are casualties of war, but in various ways they are all victims of the system.

The first two are very satisfactory portraits, since we receive mainly an external view of them. Whatever goes on inside them is conveyed in terms of action; the reader need not concern himself with complications of motive or sensibility. Andrews, however, comes through more in terms of thought and emotion than of action. And his actions are not convincing: they appear forced or irrational, existing primarily for the sake of proving a point. Worse still, he takes the novel over toward the middle and wrests it from its logical course. Instead of continuing as an objective account of men caught and broken by the war machine, the narrative becomes a conventional account of one man's misfortune, a variant of the hackneyed theme of the sensitive soul destroyed by the unfeeling world.

Over a fifth of the text relates Andrews' months in Paris as a member of the Sorbonne detachment. In theory this section about life outside the machine, especially as it describes the euphoria of encountering Paris for the first time, is justified as a contrast—freedom versus servitude, sensibility versus the freezing of human feeling and individuality—but Andrews uses freedom so badly as to undermine the whole statement. The reader is forced to an identification with him which makes his fate harrowing and personal, but upon reflection the reader can only conclude that Andrews is a fool, something of a neurotic, lacking in any saving common sense with which to protect himself, and therefore doomed to disaster in any kind of social situation. The instant such a judgment is made the burden of guilt is shifted from the army to the man, and the overall statement of the novel is impaired. It ceases to be a document of broad validity and becomes a dubious and unconvincing case study.

During his stay in Paris, Andrews is a relatively free agent, though he has to wear the hated uniform and must salute any officers he meets. It is his impetuous going off to Chartres without a pass that gets him into trouble. As he makes his fatal descent, it is almost as though he wants to be a victim, a suggestion heightened by the clumsy symbolism of his musical composition entitled "John Brown's Body." It is possible, of course, to see in this a sophisticated perspective of irony, a statement that the army, which puts men in servitude, actually frees them to be what they inherently are, vengeful assassin in the case of Chrisfield, neurotic misfit in the case of Andrews, merely accelerating the process of what they must painfully become. If this irony is present, however, it modifies the antimilitary thrust of the book and says no more than that men become what they must be wherever they are.

Serious as these structural and conceptual flaws

are, *Three Soldiers* is worthy of respect for its picture of war and its tact in presentation of documentary materials. Like *One Man's Initiation*, it is a mosaic of vignettes, in this case so extensive as to catch a great variety of situations and nuances of response. The opening picture of men at attention becoming a crowd of individuals upon dismissal, only to re-form to march to chow, and again to become one of many identical khaki rows as retreat is sounded, sets the tone of the entire work in an effective but unemphatic way. In the lives of the soldiers there is a constant tension between their robot life as soldiers and their desires, their memories, their fugitive and often pitiful efforts to be themselves. Also in the first chapter there arises the possibility of insubordination: a soldier in the guard house for punching an officer in the jaw escapes. Fuselli has a nightmare in which he does the same thing. Another recurrent theme, the pious platitudes of the noncombatants, is enunciated softly in Fuselli's ir-ritated memory of a draft board official. In introducing Andrews, the author places emphasis on humiliation and thought-deadening routine: standing naked and forgotten for physical examination, washing windows or picking up cigarette butts day after day, being con-sistently treated as an object.

Three Soldiers makes its way in logical progres-sion through training camp, embarkation camp, troop ship, and behind-the-lines activities to actual combat. However, this is not a blood-and-gore novel. As a non-combatant himself the author confines his narrative to what he has experienced and does not fake material for the sake of completeness. What he follows with scrupulous detail is the soldiers' growing awareness of the hollowness of official rhetoric, their mild culture shock (these unlettered men domesticate Argonne Forest into "Oregon Forest"; they complain because there are no milk bars in Dijon), a more and more overt xenophobia, and a deepening nostalgia for home. Out of this complex of responses comes a definite moral erosion: numerous shamefaced sexual encounters with grubby women in grubby premises followed, as Dos Passos indicates elsewhere, by remorseful prophylaxis. There is also resort to the insensibility of drunkenness and a growing disposition to scrounge and pillage. None of this is presented with the force of an indictment: these are merely facts of wartime experience sufficiently important to be noted.

The progression of discomfort and of decay of moral attitudes is presented by means of a high concentration of sensory experience: fatigue, the weight of packs, the chilling sweat of fear, loss of orientation, shell bursts, smells, the texture of hard, sour crab apples, frogs in a pond, fledgling swallows on the floor after their nests have been destroyed, the sight of a dead officer in a limousine. Response varies with the personality of the perceiver. No one overreacts. In this part of the novel there is no false note, no gratuitous or touristic addition. Nature description, while frequent, is fragmentary, casual. There are no set pieces ironically juxtaposing the tranquillity of nature and the horror of war.

In contrast to this restraint the Paris section jars. Andrews' experiences come in broad conceptual blocks, not in mosaic bits. On his walk from the railroad station he takes a guided tour, seeing and responding in stereotypes, managing to bring all the major landmarks of Paris into his field of vision. It is this change in the handling of perception that signals a change in the direction of the novel: an inductive massing of sense data gives way to an arbitrary choice of events leading the character to a predetermined end.

One of the virtues of this work is its avoidance of a stereotyped contrast between officers and men which has plagued later war novels. Officers appear only incidentally, evoking various responses from the enlisted men but occupying only the periphery of their vision. In contrast the YMCA men and chaplains are stereotyped, become caricatures as their remarks are confined to a few repeated banal utterances. They are allowed no sincerity, dignity, or masculinity.

Three elements in this early novel point forward to the mature works. Trivial but significant is the use of contemporary songs, documentary in that they are what the soldiers sang, but also broadly evocative of time and place and feeling. More important is the novelist's control of dialogue. Each soldier speaks his particular kind of language, cleaned up a bit but very accurate. Most important of all is the fact that the major characters tend to be types rather than individuals. They embody characteristic states, or attitudes, rather than significant particular responses. At this point in his writing Dos Passos was not yet committed to the precise kind of characterization he wished to employ. He started with stereotypes but allowed John Andrews to become an individual. Yet over all we can discern a disposition not to render characters fully but to give them the outlines and functions of figures in a frieze.

Dos Passos worked on *Three Soldiers* in Paris in the spring of 1919 while he was relieved of military duties so that he could attend courses at the Sorbonne.

When he had completed it, he sent it to his London publishers, who called it "a fine piece of realism, and a powerful antimilitarist document," but turned it down. In all the book had fourteen rejections before it was accepted. Even then there were difficulties. The editors told the author to cut out the smut. The author protested that "all I'd done was put down the soldiers' talk the way they talked it," but his protests were unavailing. "In the end I told them to do what they goddamn pleased with it. I was going to take the advance and get the hell out"—which he did by sailing for Europe and disappearing into the Caucasus and the Middle East. When he reached Beirut at the end of 1921, he discovered he was famous. The book was selling well and he was deluged with reviews. "Some people wanted me lynched, others were for setting up a statue."

In spite of this auspicious beginning Dos Passos had not clearly found his direction. In fact, he backslid in a distressing way, trying to consolidate his reputation as new authors often do by publishing earlier, and inferior, works which are better left in oblivion. Though not published until 1923, *Streets of Night* belongs to the period of green apprenticeship and is a depressing indication of the path the author might have followed if he had remained in the cocoon of faded preciosity. The novel is abstract, conventionally symbolic, and bloodless, setting up a contrast between those who are afraid of life and those who plunge into it and try to meet it on its own terms. Fanshawe, an instructor in fine arts at Harvard, is a typical aesthete, tied to his mother, fearing sex, living in the Italian renaissance. He is attracted to Nan, whose refuge is music, who shares his dream of walling oneself away from the ugliness and lockstep conformity of the actual world, and who is put off by sex to such an extent that she breaks her engagement with him.

He goes off to war as a Red Cross captain, is tempted for a moment by real life (a prostitute in Palermo), but makes the safe choice of "Exit to Massachusetts Avenue and the College Yard, and the museum and tea with professors' wives. . . . And I'll go back and go to and fro to lectures with a notebook under my arm, and now and then in the evening, when I haven't any engagement, walk into Boston through terrible throbbing streets and think for a moment I have Nan and Wenny with me, and that we are young, leansouled people out of the Renaissance, ready to divide life like a cake with our strong hands." The countertheme is represented by Wenny, David Wendell, a romantic who repudiates culture, saying, "God, I'd rather rot in Childs' dairy lunches. Culture's mummifying the corpse with scented preservatives. Better let it honestly putrefy, I say." He encounters real life in the person of Whitey, a down-and-outer, won't or can't carry through with a prostitute, and in the end commits suicide, which rather negates the claims of real life.

The novel offers opposing images, which by repetition define the issue: "Pico della Mirandola riding into Florence in the time of lilies" for the cloistered aesthetic state, and young Greek gods to suggest pagan openness to sensual experience. The Boston group have a tropistic tendency toward Florence, Siena, fifteenth-century Italy in general, that is, toward life sterilized and safely removed from the present. They resent the "wretched Irish politicians" who run things, are offended by "muckers," repudiate Freud because "civilized people don't let themselves think about those subjects," and in general warn themselves against being "too eager about anything." They have in their midst the appalling example of Mabel Worthington, who ran off with a common workman and is glowing and unashamed in her sexual fulfillment. They avert their eyes from common people: "Under baggy blue shirts the muscles of arms and shoulders moved tautly. A smell of sweat and rank pipes came from them." They shudder in disgust when a cemetery caretaker tells of the goings on in his domain: "It'ld fair surprise ye to see the mashin' and the spoonin' that goes on in the most high-class cemeteries." All this had recently been more tersely and more vividly expressed by T. S. Eliot in his early poems where, for example, "women come and go talking of Michelangelo" and "life is measured out in coffee spoons." Dos Passos' novel states a recognizable human dilemma, but in unexciting and hackneyed terms. His Bostonians are conventionally anemic; his real life is nothing but a few recognizable pictures at an exhibition.

The same criticism must be directed at *A Pushcart at the Curb*, a collection of poems published in 1922, verse that belongs to the author's salad days of touristic emotion, though the "Quai de Tournelle" section derives from the months in Paris in 1919 when he was writing *Three Soldiers* and had presumably moved beyond sentimental prettiness. As the title suggests, the poems seek out the picturesque in foreign settings. They are modest and uninflated, but they show no awareness that a revolution in poetry had been going on for the past ten years. He published no more poetry as such, but his later novels generally incorporate long, incantatory free-verse interludes,

suggesting both Walt Whitman and Archibald Mac-
Leish but failing of poetic intensity and condensation.

As indicated earlier, Dos Passos also had his fling
at writing plays. While his interest in the theater was
as much social as literary, he did write three plays
which are, in their way, important for their attempt to
do something original in that form. His first play, *The
Garbage Man* (mentioned as early as 1918 and produced in 1925 by the Harvard Dramatic Club under
the title *The Moon Is a Gong*), is an experimental
effort to portray the life of the Twenties in an expressionistic manner and has something in common with
Manhattan Transfer by reason of its kaleidoscopic for-
mat. Tom and Jane—Everyman and Everywoman—
go through a series of trite, though catastrophic, experiences in a world which is a cultural and intellectual
wasteland. At the end they are swept away by the
Garbage Man, blood brother to the Button Molder in
Ibsen's *Peer Gynt*. The discontinuity of the play makes
it hard to follow. The individual scenes are sometimes
interesting, sometimes opaque. Over all, it lacks co-
herence and has only visual appeal.

Airways, Inc. (1928) was the last production of
the New Playwrights' Theatre before it collapsed. It
develops a contrast between the little people and the
coercive forces of capitalist society: jerrybuilt housing,
wage slavery, corporate sharp practice, strike breaking
(a Jewish labor leader goes to the chair, recalling the
Sacco-Vanzetti case), the tawdry enjoyments of the
young, the deprivation of the old, cant phrases and
attitudes that cripple thought and action—these are
the content. The most interesting dimension of the
play, though confused in presentation, comes in the
figure of the Professor, a European revolutionary

whose best friend sold him out. His comments make the spectator realize that all this has happened before, that history is a repetitious treadmill and exploitation the common fate of man, which undermines the play's polemic immediacy.

The third and longest of these plays, *Fortune Heights*, was written about the same time. It was never produced in the United States but appears to have been put on in Russia. It is a depression play in advance of the depression, focusing on a real-estate promotion scheme in a vague locale on a national highway where the extent of the dream actually realized is represented by an unprepossessing filling station. The latter is the locus for the coming and going of a large and varied cast of people who are rootless, poverty-stricken, and without any system of human values. At the end the service-station owner and his family have been evicted and the property has been repossessed. New owners come in, imbued with their own dreams. The same sorry round of inhumanity and greed is about to be played over again.

All three plays are in fact more novelistic than dramatic. They are diffuse; they practice no economy; they have little of the heightened tension which is the basis of drama. The characters are stereotypes who somehow do not come even half alive, as they do in the novels. Both the scattershot expressionism of presentation and the stereotyped doctrinal conceptions in plot and character militate against these works as plays. There is none of the poignancy or illumination of tragedy, though they are clearly intended to point up the tragic nature of the times. There is more drama in the vignettes of *Manhattan Transfer* than there is in these plays, just as there is more poetry in the "Camera

Eye" sections of *U.S.A.* than is to be found in Dos Passos' formal efforts at poetry. By trial and error he found that conventional literary forms were not for him. By good luck he found his medium in what he ultimately called the "contemporary chronicle."

3

A Slice of Life

While the cross section was by no means Dos Passos' invention, with *Manhattan Transfer* (1925) he brought it to a perfection not matched by any of his predecessors. At the same time he created the paramount novel of the big city. This accomplishment represented the full implementation of nineteenth-century realism in the American novel, though with a difference.

What he had before him as examples were works as various as Flaubert's *Madame Bovary* and *L'Éducation sentimentale*, Zola's *L'Assommoir* and *Pot-Bouille*, the contemporary novels of Benito Pérez Galdós, and most immediately James Joyce's *Ulysses*. It must be noted emphatically that there was no American cross-section novel of magnitude before this work, and that it came out some years before Jules Romains' *Les Hommes de bonne volonté*, with which it and *U.S.A.* have often been compared. Certainly Dos Passos learned from his predecessors, but he did not draw slavishly from them. Rather he took the salient characteristics of this form as it had been variously developed and gave it his own unique embodiment.

This type of novel does not have fixed rules but can be described as a kind of mosaic, or, better, a revolving stage that presents a multitude of scenes and characters which, taken together, convey a sense of the life of a given milieu and by extension give the tone of contemporary life generally. The strategy is to move the reader through a varied series of actions involving a broad and representative cast of characters. It is inductive, a sort of Gallup poll, by which the meaning is the sum of all the parts. Thus *Madame Bovary* seeks to render, as indicated by its subtitle "Moeurs de Province," what it is like to live in the provinces, Zola's

38

L'Assommoir and *Pot-Bouille* what it is like to live in Parisian proletarian and middle-class milieux respectively. The Galdós novels concentrate on the life of Madrid, ranging through all social classes and sections of the city. Finally, there is the example of *Ulysses*, where the dominant narrative interest in Leopold Bloom and Stephen Dedalus is supplemented by a quick succession of incidental scenes giving a sense of Dublin life, most notably in the so-called "Wandering Rocks" episode at the center of the novel.

This type of novel almost automatically exhibits unity of place. (*War and Peace* is the great exception.) It handles the dimension of time in a variety of ways. Dos Passos opts here for the predominant time pattern, that of a period of years approximating a generation, a sufficient span of growth and change to demonstrate the effects of a given milieu. While *Manhattan Transfer* is not a chronicle of public events to the same extent as *U.S.A.* is, it does have a sufficient time scheme to assist the reader's orientation. The novel begins about 1904—there are references to the Roosevelt-Parker contest for the presidency in that year—and continues to a less determinate point in the mid-Twenties. We are reminded as the novel comes to an end that Congo Jake had come to America twenty years before, that "Lady Be Good" is a current song hit, but there is no reference to events of such public importance as the Sacco-Vanzetti case or the Teapot Dome scandal.

This lack of detailed chronological reference is important in that it directs attention not to people's subjection to major external forces such as wars, ideologies, and economic crises, but to something more subtle, a changing psychosocial ambiance, a revolution

in life styles and values. This approach is signaled by
the vignette which closes the first chapter: "A small
bearded bandylegged man in a derby" contemplates
an advertisement presenting the cleanshaven face of
King C. Gillette and, clenching his fists and throwing
back his shoulders, the man daringly enters a shop and
buys a safety razor. When his wife and daughters
reach home, for a moment they do not recognize him.
Thus we are told that a new era in American life has
begun. It is interesting that World War I, which is
generally considered to have been the prime causative
factor in changing American mores (and which is elsewhere carefully analyzed by Dos Passos), is here
passed over in a few sentences and by the evocation of
a few slogans. The reasons for change are relatively
unimportant; it is the experience and the fact of
change that is under examination.

Before we can analyze the nature of that experience, it is necessary to look at the cross section of
characters who undergo it. In this kind of novel we do
not know when a personage first appears whether he
will have an important role or not. It is only by his
persistence in the narrative and the emphasis he receives that we can judge his weight. In *Manhattan
Transfer* there are four clear categories of character.
At the bottom of the scale are incidental, often anon-
ymous, individuals whose situation may best be described as a thematic supplement to the main narrative: for example, at the very beginning a group of
bewildered immigrants, or at the end an old derelict
weeping in the street. Next in importance are those
characters who appear in several scenes but who are
not present throughout and are not closely connected
with other characters. Such a case is Bud Korpenning,

who comes to New York as the novel opens, appears in eight scenes, and commits suicide at the end of Part I. Toward the end of the work we have two similar cases, Anna Cohen and Dutch Robertson, little people, the disaster of whose lives adds poignancy to the general statement.

Ideally a cross-section novel should have no protagonist, should make its case by following a considerable number of personages of fairly equal importance and representativeness. Before coming to this, the second level, however, we must acknowledge that in this instance Dos Passos does concentrate on two major figures, Ellen Thatcher and Jimmy Herf. It is around them that the second-level characters gravitate. Some have a direct attachment, like that of Oglethorpe to Ellen, or of James Merivale to Jimmy. Some are disconnected parallels, as is the case with the architect Philip Sandbourne. All are to be seen as following similar courses in their search for success in an environment that is hostile or indifferent. The reader cannot escape asking whether in fact these figures are sufficiently representative. The answer is ambiguous: banker, lawyer, broker, bootlegger, labor leader, architect, impresario—these are by no means a complete gamut but they do serve as an adequate sampling, though a bit out of balance by reason of the number of hangers-on in the arts who surround Ellen.

The two major characters do stand out from the mass and dominate the novel. Ellen—Elaine, Helena, depending on her mood and aspiration—is inhibited by no particular scruples in her effort to get ahead. She is not a monster, merely a self-centered woman determined to get what she wants without regard for standards of morality or convention. She first marries

Jojo Oglethorpe, a much older man, an actor and a homosexual, because she thinks he can help her become an actress. She impulsively marries Jimmy Herf in Europe during World War I and drops him when he can no longer support her. There seem to be many other men in her life. Stan Emery, whom she really loves, kills himself in a drunken frenzy. She aborts the child he has fathered. She is pursued throughout the novel by George Baldwin, an attorney with political aspirations, whom she resignedly marries at the end. The significant things in Ellen's makeup are her ambition and her egotism. Like Dreiser's Sister Carrie, she makes her way in the theater more by beauty and sex appeal than by talent. She uses people around her and discards them when they are no longer of use. The last we see of her is in a display of hardened indifference to the death of Anna Cohen in Madame Soubrine's boutique. She is one who succeeds, at the cost of petrified emotions.

The personality of Jimmy Herf is more difficult to pin down. He is, obviously, one of those partial projections of his own being that Dos Passos frequently makes. He returns to the United States as a small boy after long residence in Europe; he has no father; his mother dies when he is sixteen; he serves in the Red Cross during the war. He is by far the most sensitive and articulate of the people in the novel. However, it is a mistake to see him as directly echoing the author's experience. His function in the novel is to be odd man out, to be the uneasy seeker of a value system counter to that subscribed to by the rest, to refuse to make the compromises that worldly success demands. At the end he opts out. We last see him hitching a ride in the wasteland of the Jersey Flats.

Another way of evaluating this cross section is to ask whether it permits too much in the way of extreme cases, whether it runs to the edges of the human gamut of experience, to situations so far from the median that they are usually cut off in a sampling or poll. Bud Korpenning is such a case, not because he is a rustic adrift in New York, but because after the murder of his father he is a fugitive. Such is the case with Blackhead and Densch, not because their business fails, but because it fails to the tune of $10,000,000, thus setting them apart from the general level of mediocrity of the novel. Tony Hunter, an unhappy homosexual, is another extreme case, though noteworthy because he is the first such figure given detailed presentation in American fiction.

The lives of these people are presented discontinuously. The novel consists of some 130 scenes, the longest of which runs thirteen pages. There are no transitions, although in a few cases succeeding scenes are linked by simultaneity of action. Most of the sections carry forward the experiences of the more important characters, but at the very beginning there are seven scenes that are incidental or thematic, and at the end this device is used again. The importance of the main characters can be gauged by the frequency of their appearance, Ellen (or her father) in thirty-six scenes, Jimmy Herf in twenty-six, George Baldwin in sixteen, Gus McNiel in fourteen. This broad and varied scenic presentation indicates the basically inductive nature of the cross-section technique. The author provides what he thinks is an adequate sampling; the reader contemplates it, as he would the people whom he encounters in real life. He is left to draw his own conclusions without overt authorial intervention or moralizing, though we cannot deny that there is an intelligence, however unobtrusive, which has chosen and arranged the elements on which the reader is to pass judgment.

What generally occurs in realistic novels is that lives go downhill; there is a high incidence of disappointment and failure. Dos Passos conforms to this pattern. He sets his representative group in a given milieu, records their activities over a period of years, and permits little deviation from a pessimistic downward curve. He shows, as did his master Flaubert, that most people fail and that the ostensible success of a few must, by any reasonable standard, be considered failure. For example, Gus McNiel, a milkman, by the fortunate incapacitation he suffers in an accident is diverted into labor-union activities. His role as a big shot is hedged with ambiguity. Congo Jake arrives at wealth and a Park Avenue apartment and assumes his proper impressive name of Armand Duval. Yet his situation is precarious. He has arrived by being a bootlegger. Any day he may be arrested, convicted, and sentenced to Atlanta. George Baldwin, who takes advantage of McNiel's accident to get his start as a lawyer (and with equal opportunism enjoys McNiel's wife for a season), eventually goes into politics, cynically assuming the label of reform candidate but destined to be the puppet of the big corporations. James Merivale, Jimmy's cousin and foil, follows the straight and narrow path of a banker, watching his every gesture, denying himself any spontaneity of action, accepting even a legally dubious marriage for his sister because of the advantage to be gained from her husband's connections. These are the apparent winners.

The rest of the characters are obvious losers.

Heading the list is Joe Harland, a Herf and Merivale relative, once a big man on Wall Street, who goes downhill rapidly after his first disgraceful appearance in one of the opening scenes: drunkard, debtor, scrounger, night watchman, inevitably soon to be a Bowery derelict. In their way Blackhead and Densch parallel his situation. After the collapse of their business the former lives the life of an exile in Marienbad on money belonging to his creditors, presumably in danger of extradition; the latter evades his obligations by diverting money to his daughter's safety deposit box. As he dies of a heart attack, his houseboy spits in his face. Each has become a kind of nonperson. Also in parallel is Jake Silverman, a promoter, who is haled off to jail for his fraudulent stock promotions, leaving his inamorata Rosie to hock everything portable and beat it. Phil Sandbourne, with a vision of architectural grandeur, is pinned to the drafting board of unimaginative commercial builders. Stan Emery, born to every advantage, lives the life of a psychopathic hobbledehoy and dies through drunken misadventure, a playboy to the end.

Beyond these people of some position and substance are the born losers. The whole pathetic group around Ellen at her boarding house are hangers-on in the theater, or more precisely in show business, since there is no evidence that they have any talent or genuine vision of art. The most interesting of them is Nevada Jones, who, married to Congo Jake after a spotted past, has the determination to make a go of her marriage. The marginal economic men and women are represented by Bud Korpenning, unskilled and without resources in the big city; Dutch Robertson, a returned veteran who resorts to crime in desperation,

and his girl friend Francie; Anna Cohen, whom we see
in a variety of marginal jobs; Joe O'Keefe, first an
obsequious follower of McNiel, then trying to make it
on his own by means of a bonus racket for veterans.
Behind all these, their hands uplifted in supplication,
are the nameless, helpless ones, usually immigrants,
battered by life in Europe, battered and beaten again
in New York.

There is a fair amount of commentary on the nature of success and failure made by the characters
themselves. To this extent the novel has an ideological
or social focus, for the point seems to be that success
as conceived within the existing social framework
means conformity and a kind of progressive dehumanization. Two images at the beginning of the work assert this. People emerging from the ferry are "crushed
and jostling like apples fed down a chute into a press;"
and the newborn baby Ellen Thatcher "squirmed in
the cotton-wool feebly like a knot of earthworms." Un-
like most realists, Dos Passos does not make capital of
the reductionist nature of the latter image. He does
not in the manner of Zola and Dreiser compare his
people to lower forms of life. What he insists on in this
novel is the reduction of human beings to something
mechanical. The heading of Chapter V, "Steamroller,"
suggests this process. This is the culminating chapter
of Part I, in which the subsidence of hope and joy is
quadruply indicated by the death of Jimmy Herf's
mother, Ellen's marriage, Emile's crass opportunism,
and Bud Korpenning's suicide. These mechanical images are frequent throughout the work. People are fed
into revolving doors; they walk on a treadmill; they
are jiggling corpses in a subway car. Jimmy sees himself in his job as reporter as no more than an automa-

ton. Ellen, as she capitulates to conformity, plays with phrases like mechanical doll, talking doll, mechanical toy, porcelain figurine, frozen photograph. This is actuality as the two principal figures perceive it, and as the minor figures experience it. It is an actuality to which Ellen submits and from which Jimmy flees.

In contrast to this implacable process of the steamroller there is a world of dreams, which envisions some form of escape. Authorial omniscience generally stops short of presenting interior states except for a stylized rendition of secret aspiration. Just before his suicide, Bud, recognizing that he "Cant go nowhere now," promptly switches to a daydream of Alderman Bud "riding in a carriage to City Hall . . . through rows of men waving cigars, bowing, doffing brown derbies." Joe Harland, snug in his nightwatchman's lean-to, for a moment sees himself once more "in a dress-suit wearing a top hat with an orchid in his buttonhole." Jimmy Herf, out of a job and sitting in Washington Square, broods on his failure: "In Yonkers, I buried my boyhood, in Marseilles with the wind in my face I dumped my calf years into the harbor. Where in New York shall I bury my twenties? Maybe they were deported and went out to sea on the Ellis Island ferry singing the International." He then embodies his feelings in an imaginary newspaper article entitled "Deported" and in a court scene resembling Joyce's "Circe" episode that seeks to dramatize contemporary values.

James Merivale, an unimaginative man, dreams of a testimonial dinner offered by the American Bankers Association to him as president of the Bank & Trust Company. Even such a minor character as Anna Cohen dreams of her boyfriend Elmer "in a dinner coat, with eartabs, tall as Valentino, strong as Doug.

The Revolution is declared. The Red Guard is march-
ing up Fifth Avenue. Anna in golden curls with a little
kitten under her arm leans with him out of the tallest
window." These dreams are obviously ironic, posi-
tioned as they are at points of disappointment or disaster in the lives of the dreamers. Anna's, for example,
comes just seconds before she is horribly burned to
death.

The other exception to the practice of allowing
dialogue to carry the narrative and reveal the characters' mental states comes with the development of
Jimmy Herf and less·frequently of Ellen Thatcher.
Here the technique is usually indirect interior mono-
logue, that is, thoughts conveyed in the third person
rather than the first. These passages show the strong
influence of Joyce's *Ulysses* in their intricate verbal
play. For example:

Ellen in her new dress of Black Watch plaid mummy'd
bought at Hearn's walked down the asphalt path kicking
her toes in the air. There was a silver thistle brooch on the
shoulder of the new dress of Black Watch plaid mummy'd
bought at Hearn's. Elaine of Lammermoor was going to be
married. The Betrothed. Wangnaan nainainai, went the
bagpipes going through the ɪye. The man on the bench has
a patch over his eye. A watching black patch. A black
watching patch. The kidnapper of the Black Watch, among
the rustling shrubs kidnappers keep their Black Watch.

Such a passage is no longer straight interior mono-
logue but involves a verbal play which goes beyond
what the character would be thinking. There are many
such echoes of *Ulysses*, recognizable by verbal technique or sometimes by actual content. "From Liver-
pool, British steamer Raleigh . . ." recalls Joyce's

"Rosevean from Bridgewater with bricks." There is an unidentified character sorrowing over the death of her husband in the General Slocum disaster in 1904, one of the few non-Irish events referred to in Joyce's novel.

These experiments do not, on the whole, greatly change the texture of the work. We see almost entirely through the eyes of the impersonal narrator. But he is selective, even impressionistic. Characters rarely appear in full outline: a salient characteristic stands for the whole, and nine times out of ten that characteristic is a hat. The sensory experience of his people is dominated by smell; the novel contains an immense catalogue of the smells of the city. Auditory and tactile sensations are comparatively rare. Sight concentrates on sky, light, flashing color, silhouettes of light and darkness.

Manhattan Transfer goes beyond traditional realism in other important respects. It has often been called expressionistic; that is, it attempts to externalize essences, meanings, significant realities that lurk beneath the surface of observed reality. In a play, costume, sets, lighting, and discordant apposition of sensory elements generally are the means of bringing this out. In a novel the techniques available are less varied; the prime means are linguistic and imagistic. Out of these may come a thematic insistence on some element of meaning that inheres in the data presented but is not readily apparent without such emphasis, or there may be an intrusion of elements that are discordant in the realistic texture and therefore force the reader to seek out their significance. A simple instance in *Manhattan Transfer* is the songs or fragments of songs introduced. Of course, they have a realistic appropriateness in that they are data of the times. They help move us chronologically through the years of the novel, and they are a pointed notation of the vanities and inanities of that era.

Much more important are certain recurring materials bearing on the city itself. It is in these that we find the expressionistic nature of the work. It is immediately apparent that New York City as a physical entity is not going to be treated realistically. The vignette introducing Chapter I is poetic, though full of realistic detail. The second clearly goes beyond realistic statement:

There were Babylon and Nineveh: they were built of brick. Athens was gold marble columns. Rome was held up on broad arches of rubble. In Constantinople the minarets flame like great candles round the Golden Horn. . . . Steel, glass, tile, concrete will be the materials of the skyscrapers. Crammed on the narrow island the millionwindowed buildings will jut glittering, pyramid on pyramid like the white cloudhead above a thunderstorm.

In this passage there is an ambiguity that pervades the novel. On the one hand, New York City takes its place among the great cities of civilization, the highest embodiment of human aspiration in the material world. Their materials are both rare and common—gold and rubble. But implicit in the roll call is the fact that the older cities have fallen, have gone back to rubble, whatever their onetime brilliance. The skyscraper functions as an embodiment of contemporary aspiration. Phil Sandbourne dreams of a new artistic form with new materials; Stan Emery, in his habitual euphoric intoxication, just before his death repeats the passage just quoted, joins it to a song recalling the

Flood, and exclaims, "Kerist I wish I was a skyscraper."

Throughout the novel there is a recurring image of a fire engine. It appears to Emery going "licketysplit trailing a droning sirenshriek." He has an obsessive vision of skyscrapers going up in flames, flames, flames. He turns on the gas jet, pours kerosene, strikes matches. This linking of skyscraper metropolis and consuming fire has been carefully prepared. Chapter Two, which enunciates the gold, brick, rubble theme, also contains an account of a tenement fire. Ellen Thatcher's mother remembers "that terrible Chicago theater fire." When Jimmy Herf returns to New York as a little boy he encounters a fire engine. Chapter Four of Part II is entitled "Fire Engine" and prepares for Stan's death two chapters later. A fire engine roars by as Ellen decides to have his child aborted. The prologue to the first chapter of Part III likens the war to the Apocalypse in terms of "typhus, cholera, shrapnel, insurrection, death in fire, death in water, death in hunger, death in mud." Later on a crazed prophet tells two small boys of the fire and brimstone and earthquake and tidal wave that will bring the tall buildings crashing down. It is a doomed city, and by extension so are the people in it.

The images of flashing light and color, which are the chief means of describing the city, are also ambiguous. They are a lure, an aspiration, a promise of an Arabian Nights fairyland, but they are also a delusion. What is so fair and promising becomes an agent of disappointment and destruction. Ellis Island and the Statue of Liberty, which frequently figure in this imagery as beacons of hope and freedom, betray their promises. New York is a lodestone, a focus of aspiration which by essential cosmic irony is bound to disappoint. There is a double movement within the novel, an almost heliotropic drawing toward the city, as evidenced in the beginning by the arrival of Bud Korpenning, Jimmy Herf, Michel and Congo Jake, and a body of unnamed immigrants; and a countermovement, a frenetic desire to get away. The city attracts by its bigness—we learn at the beginning that New York has just become the second most populous urban agglomeration in the world—but that bigness is stultifying because of its indifference, its reduction of people to things. It is a vision of beauty and proud artistry which, like all things created by man, is destined to decay over the long perspective of time, but it is also in the short run ugly and ruinous, tawdry and evil-smelling. Through these imagistic emphases and contrasts we get the essence of New York City as siren and destroyer, promising and not keeping her promises, as in the case of the immigrants who are destroyed or who are deported because of their belief in freedom.

This novel contains little of what we call social criticism in terms of institutional malfunction or ideological argument. War as a means of controlling the restless masses, the uneven hand of justice, the non-existent chances of the working stiff, the primacy of money, indifference to genuine artistic vision—all these criticisms are incidentally voiced out of the mouths of various characters, but in no sustained or doctrinaire way. It is changing mores and moral values, without much concern for the forces that produce such change, that are the objects of observation in *Manhattan Transfer*. This work goes much further than Dreiser's novels in its assertion of a gap between official and actual morality. It is much more probing than Sinclair Lewis' satiric accounts of the pressures of conformity.

The cleanshaven man at the beginning heralds a new era. The new dances, the jazz tunes, the incidental slogans give the flavor of the times. Beneath that surface the reader is constantly confronted with several major currents of change. Interestingly enough, two important aspects of the new society are left out, the automobile and the movies. We do see the transition from horsedrawn fire engines to those powered by combustion engines, but there is no recognition of the new mobility of the automobile age, chiefly, it may be assumed, because of the restricted geographical setting. The absence of the movies is harder to account for. This is a serious oversight, since the world of make-believe and wish fulfillment provided by the movies would be a natural reinforcement for the tawdry life of illusion with which the novel deals.

There are three major shifts in social morality which this work continually stresses. One is prohibition, another is gangsterism in labor and business, a third is the sexual revolution. Prohibition becomes more than a background element when the Herfs return from Europe after the war, laden with contraband bottles even in the baby's bassinette. Speakeasies and the various evasions of the law against public drinking are shown as part of the new mores and need no comment. Toward the end of the novel there is a detailed highjacking scene on Long Island which Jimmy witnesses and in which Congo Jake is a principal. It is by such activities outside the law that Jake has risen to affluence and a degree of distinction, evidence of the easy and dubious ways by which it is possible to rise in the new society, in the impersonal and amoral city. Racketeering is closely allied to this. We see Gus McNiel achieving power in politics; we see Joe O'Keefe's attempts to coerce Joe Harland to go out on strike. The possibilities of power and coercion are clearly suggested, but they are neither developed nor judged as they are to be in Dos Passos' later and more tendentious novels.

Most attention is given to the sexual revolution, again without moralizing. Ellen Thatcher is a liberated woman. She uses men and discards them. Scenes of sexual intimacy among minor characters are numerous, served up as a staple of modern existence. By its matter-of-fact acceptance of sexual license, by its de-romanticizing of sex and portraying it as a casual appetite, this novel is a milestone in the depiction of American life. Nothing before it had been so down to earth, so unpruriently straightforward, not even Dreiser's *Sister Carrie*.

Dos Passos came back from one of his long European journeys in the early Twenties, saying he had had enough of Europe: it was time to discover his own country. *Manhattan Transfer* was part of that voyage of discovery. Except for Jimmy Herf, and possibly Stan Emery, none of the characters he presents are the type of people he knew well. He ignores the big business world of his father almost entirely; he leaves out the genuine artists and intellectuals with whom he associated. Instead he ranges widely among lower-middle-class and proletarian types. It must be admitted that they are usually two-dimensional, but within those limits they are acceptable and ring true. They bear the stamp of careful observation, though they are not imbued with that extra element of humanity that makes some fictional characters memorable. The whole novel is an attempt to encompass a segment of American life, its sights and sounds, the feeling and texture of its speech. This is carried out with cool reportorial detachment in an attempt to get it down right, and with an equally detached interest in seeing what could be done with such materials. Intelligence rules here. Passion will come later.

4

∞∞∞

"Visions . . . "

By its intricacy and by its comprehensive sweep the trilogy *U.S.A.* comes close to being the great American novel which had been the aspiration of writers since the turn of the century. It is one of the ironies of our times that when the great American novel did arrive, it turned out to be condemnatory and pessimistic rather than a celebration of the American way. Yet there is an underlying affirmation in Dos Passos' denial. The American dream, battered and corrupted by men of ill will, or little will, still manifests itself—though in anguish—not completely stifled by the trappings of empire and the machinations of self-interest that the author describes.

What first aroused the enthusiasm of readers and critics was the technical virtuosity of the work. Dos Passos was clearly the heir of Balzac, Zola, and Galdós in his attempt to mirror contemporary society—as he was the competitor of Jules Romains, whose *Hommes de bonne volonté* was appearing during the same span of years. It is equally evident that the idea of multiple perspectives is something he owed to *Ulysses*. But the techniques he employed and the balance of elements he achieved are his own and stamp him as the last of the great inventors in the field of the social novel. He welded together four separate, even disparate, types of material, each of which is necessary to the statement the novel ultimately makes. He spoke of this as his "four way conveyer system," which is apt enough, since four kinds of ore are being mined simultaneously.

One of the problems of the novelist attempting to mirror social actuality is how to include a sufficient body of data to give the basic tone or temper of the times as background to the necessarily particular experience of fictional characters. Balzac, Zola, and Galdós

did this largely by repetition; that is, within the loosely
associated novels of their series they subjected characters from various walks of life to the same basic
determining and limiting forces. They were generally
content with only a brief suggestive notation of public
events. Even though change was their subject, there
was something relatively static about their social back-
drop. Later novelists, like James T. Farrell and John
Steinbeck, attempted to remedy this deficiency. Steinbeck, in *The Grapes of Wrath,* by means of inter-
calated chapters which are poetic or rhetorical rather
than directly documentary, both sets the social background and incorporates change as one of the dimensions of that background.

Dos Passos meets the problem by an invention
that he calls the "Newsreel." There are sixty-eight such
sections fairly evenly distributed among the three
novels of the trilogy. These sections are a mixture of
newspaper headlines, fragments of news stories, and
bits and pieces of popular songs. They rarely run over
two pages; a few are very short. They are typographi-
cally arresting with their headline type and their inset
lines of verse. Their function is threefold: they precisely date the narrative action; they arouse a feeling
for the time in question; and they frequently have a
thematic or ironic impact.

In each volume of the trilogy the first and last
Newsreels are of particular importance for all of the
reasons just stated. *The 42nd Parallel* (1930) opens
with a proclamation by way of headlines that the new
century has begun. The repetitive banality of these
statements becomes ludicrous, a tone that carries over
to Senator Albert J. Beveridge's claim that "The twentieth century will be American. American thought will

dominate it. American progress will give it color and direction. American deeds will make it illustrious." In counterpoint there is obvious triviality: "Society Girls Shocked: Danced with Detectives," and venality: "Officials Know Nothing of Vice." Then follows an ominous note of prophecy with mention of the disastrous Boer War and the nascent American empire: a jingle from the Cuban campaign; a headline: "Claims Islands for All Time"; and finally a song from the Philippine campaign, bits of which appear throughout the section, culminating with a warning of the cost of empire:

> There's been many a good man murdered in the Philippines
>   Lies sleeping in some lonesome grave.

The final Newsreel of the volume is shorter and less complex. The declaration of war in April 1917 is announced in headlines; there are lines from the popular song "Over There," reference to the fact that the Colt Firearms Company has increased profits by 259 per cent, and two headlines: "Plan Legislation to Keep Colored People from White Areas" and "Abusing Flag to Be Punished." The long-range implications of war are set down without comment.

The opening theme of *1919* (1932) is one of a capitalistic system both intoxicated by opportunity and frightened by lurking dangers: the New York Stock Exchange is now the only free market in the world; vast quantities of money are pouring in from abroad; but "Europe [is] reeking with murder and the lust of rapine, aflame with the fires of revolution." The concluding Newsreel is savage: "the placards borne by the radicals were taken away from them, their clothing torn and eyes blackened before the service and ex-

service men had finished with them." "Machineguns
Mow Down Mobs in Knoxville." Juxtaposed to this
violence is the phrase "America I love you." The war is
over. Its fruits are becoming known.

In *The Big Money* (1936) the first Newsreel
comes after a narrative section. It contains much less
detonative material than the foregoing: a line from
"The St. Louis Blues," headlines about a daylight rob-
bery, observations about automobiles and social status.
Though the word is not used, this is President Hard-
ing's "normalcy." The contrast provided by the final
Newsreel is dramatic: "Wall Street Stunned" (the
stock market crash); "Police Turn Machine Guns on
Colorado Mine Strikers Kill 5 Wound 40;" "Rescue
Crews Try to Upend Ill-fated Craft While Waiting for
Pontoons." All this is interspersed with lines from the
saga of the ill-fated Casey Jones, whose locomotive is
hell-bent for destruction. Finally there are the hollow
soothing words of the President at the dedication of
the Bok carillon in Florida, a scene of peace and promise already denied by the headlines: "Steamroller in
Action against Militants," "Miners Battle Scabs."

Some of the content of the Newsreels is just
plain fun. Advertising slogans such as "Itching Gone in
One Night," the whole fulsome sequence of headlines
about Queen Marie of Romania's visit, saccharine
songs juxtaposed with serious events, all of these give
a sense of the human comedy and also bring a powerful evocation of the past to the reader who has lived
through it. Intellectually he may be aware of triviality
and folly, of stultifying forces that controlled his life,
but his emotions discount all that. It is his past, a poor
thing but his own.

The present-day reader has to ask himself what is

the enduring value of these sections, what kind of impact do they have on people who have not lived through the time portrayed? In general, popular songs wear themselves out by repetition; they rarely reappear to stir the emotions of another generation, though certain ballads like "Casey Jones," certain fighting chants of the IWW and other leftist groups, and hardcore revolutionary anthems like "The Marseillaise" and "The Internationale" do have long-term currency. The problem is even more evident when it comes to headlines and excerpts of news stories, many of which are extremely hard to pin down with the passage of time. It takes an effort of will, and some luck, to be able to recall that "Peaches" was Peaches Browning, that "The Sheik" was Rudolph Valentino, or to be able to piece together the details of the Hall-Mills murder case. Perhaps the relative inaccessibility of these materials does not matter. The author operates on the scattershot principle: some of the shots are sure to hit.

The second of Dos Passos' conveyor belts, the short biographies of actual persons, is also highly original. Living people have been used before as touchstones in novels, as objects of glorification or as objects of scorn. What is unusual here is the number and variety of the biographies and the encapsulated way in which they are presented. There are twenty-seven of them equally distributed among the three novels. They direct attention to both success and failure in the first third of the century and to major social currents of that period. By the selectivity evident in their choice it is clear that the author has here cast aside his role of objective observer and has actively intervened to influence the reader's judgment. A completely different statement would emerge if the cast of living persons were different.

There is no easy formula for classifying these figures, though, as has been indicated, they fall broadly
into groupings of good guys and bad guys, heroes and
villains, constructive and destructive human beings.
But the sketches are so imbued with irony that the
reader does not know what to expect in advance. He is
obliged to examine each sketch in its context and to be
ready for an ironic twist which will upset his expectation. The initial biography, "Lover of Mankind," is of
Eugene V. Debs, the first nationally celebrated labor
leader. This choice, and the tone in which the biography is written, constitutes an unambiguous manifesto.
Debs' aspiration is for "a world brothers might own
where everybody would split even." The section ends
with the ringing quotation: "While there is a lower
class I am of it, while there is a criminal class I am of
it, while there is a soul in prison I am not free." The
authorial voice betrays partisanship when it asks
where were Debs' brothers in 1918 "when Woodrow
Wilson had him locked up in Atlanta for speaking
against war." The central issue which is gradually to
become clear in the course of the novel is implicit in
this biography: there are two nations, men with a
sense of brotherhood like Debs and "the frockcoats
and the tophats and diamonded hostesses," the wield-
ers of power who "were afraid of him as if he had
contracted a social disease, syphilis or leprosy."

Two other biographies in the first volume rein-
force this statement. "Big Bill," that is, Big Bill Hay-
wood the IWW leader, dreamed of "building a new
society in the shell of the old"; he was the victim of the
mentality of the men who "went over with the A.E.F.
to save the Morgan loans" and "lynched the pacifists
and the pro-Germans and the wobblies and the reds
and the bolsheviks." Another idealist and victim is

"Fighting Bob" La Follette, the reformer who made Wisconsin a model state, who fought corruption and big business and "the miasmic lethargy of Washington." He was "an orator haranguing from the capitol of a lost republic."

The Luther Burbank sketch raises important questions. America is a hybrid, promising a brave new social organism, but it is threatened by intolerance of ideas, something which did not destroy Burbank but left him "puzzled." Edison's fame is undercut by the fact that he worked with men like Henry Ford and Harvey Firestone, "who never worried about mathematics or the social system or generalized philosophical concepts," and put his inventions at the service of these analphabetic masters of the capitalist system. Likewise Steinmetz, a hunchback and a genius and a socialist whose mathematical discoveries are the basis of all electrical transformers everywhere, was merely "a piece of apparatus belonging to General Electric," which indulged him in his socialist dreams but did not allow him to interfere with the stockholders' money or the directors' salaries.

Alongside these men manipulated by the system we see three of the manipulators. The most openly attacked is Minor C. Keith, builder of railroads in Central America and creator of the United Fruit Company. Andrew Carnegie, like Steinmetz an immigrant, worked hard, saved his money, and "whenever he had a million dollars he invested it . . . whenever he made a billion dollars he endowed an institution to promote universal peace always except in time of war." The most ironic sketch of all is that of William Jennings Bryan, "the boy orator of the Platte," whose silver tongue chanted indiscriminately of pacifism, prohibition, and fundamentalism; the leader of the people's crusade who became the clown in the courtroom at the monkey trial in Dayton, Tennessee, who became a barker selling real estate in Coral Gables, Florida.

This pattern is repeated in *1919*, but in *The Big Money* the biographies have a different orientation. They are illustrative of the anti-human, anti-cultural wasteland of the Twenties: Frederick W. Taylor, the inventor of the system of industrial management that reduces workmen to the status of machines (to the point of emasculation, one of the fictional characters observes); Henry Ford, chief architect of the new society produced by the automobile, whose social outlook belonged to the horse-and-buggy age; and William Randolph Hearst, a manipulator of men's minds and a vulgarizer of ideas. In Isadora Duncan and Rudolph Valentino are summed up both the inanity of pseudo-art and the vacuous enthusiasms of a vulgar public. Three biographies only are touchstones of what is useful and admirable: Thorstein Veblen, who saw through the glittering facade of conspicuous consumption and became an academic pariah for his pains; the Wright Brothers, who with single-minded devotion pioneered man's entry into the space age; and Frank Lloyd Wright, whose vision of a humane functional architecture was one of the few creative achievements of the age.

These twenty-seven portraits are in general a cruel and unsparing debunking, less cantankerous than H. L. Mencken's parallel effort but more deadly. They demand a reassessment of reputations in terms of a constant vision of a good society; they strip away the window-dressing of factitious public image. Underlying all of them is a basic question: Who were the great

men of the new century? This question cannot in fact
be answered until valid criteria of greatness are established. Dos Passos leads us to those criteria in a nega-
tive manner for the most part. The reader is brought
to see the hollowness, the sterility of many men of
popular reputation and is forced, often painfully, to
reassess unpopular personalities whom he had assumed to be beyond the pale. For all the cool, precise
succinctness of these biographies there is nothing impersonal about them. They constitute the most brilliant writing Dos Passos ever did, but that brilliance is
one of polemic thrust under the cloak of objectivity.
Not only do they set up a general value system for the
novel; they act as reflectors for the fictional personages, as in the case where the narrative of Margo
Dowling is interrupted by a biography of Valentino.

The third device invented by Dos Passos, the
"Camera Eye," is the most interesting because the
most difficult to pin down as to its function. There are
fifty-one of these sections, over half of them appearing
in the first novel. Whereas the approach of all the
other elements in the work is public and ostensibly
objective, the Camera Eyes are private and subjective.
Their style is lyrical in contrast to the dry factual presentation of the rest. Through them an unexpected
persona appears on scene, a poetic speaker who is different from the impersonal narrator and who for prac-
tical purposes must be identified with that unique individual John Dos Passos. This individual is both
representative and unique. He is the sensitive pro-
tected being who must emerge from the safety of
childhood and come to an understanding of the harsh
realities of adult life. There is a strict parallel between
his experience and that of the United States in the

twentieth century. Youth undergoes crisis when it dis-
covers that the maxims—the official verbal formulas—
on which it has been nurtured do not square with
reality. Two courses are open to meet this crisis: a
cynical capitulation to the way things are, or a radical
reassessment of traditional values and a determination
to sweep away all that is not valid at whatever cost. In
other words, the Camera Eyes provide a core of belief
and value in the midst of apparent disintegration of
value. In simplistic terms they chart the making of a
radical.

Dos Passos here mines his own experience with
virtually no resort to invention. The twenty-seven
Camera Eyes in *The 42nd Parallel* carry the speaker
through childhood and adolescence to his post-Har-
vard trip to France in 1916. Curiously enough, the
definitive end to childhood is deferred to the beginning of *1919*, when the deaths of mother and father
(separated in fact by several years) are brought together in the opening section, along with the experience of a soldier's life (largely imaginary). These experiences are described as the closing of one book and
the beginning of another, a *Vita Nuova*, "the first day
of the first month of the first year" of a new existence.

The first Camera Eye describes insecurity in a
foreign city. The second is doubly thematic, expressing
a patronizing attitude toward Negroes and windy
patriotic hyperbole. The third section echoes this class
consciousness: "workingmen and people like that la-
borers travailleurs greasers." This theme comes up
again in the seventh: in reference to muckers, Bohunks
and Polack kids who "put stones in their snowballs
write dirty words up on walls do dirty things up alleys
their folks work in the mills," an attitude that is under-

cut in the next Camera Eye by the intolerance, cruelty, and dirty words at the speaker's own select school. As the novel continues, sex, patriotism, social conscious- ness (the Lawrence, Massachusetts, street car strike), an account of a New York radical meeting where "everybody talked machineguns revolution civil liberty freedom of speech but occasionally somebody got in the way of a cop and was beaten up and shoved into a patrol wagon," and growing awareness of the evil of war—"up north they were dying in the mud and the trenches but business was good in Bordeaux"—chart the sensitivity of the speaker.

With this persona established, it is possible to limit the range of the Camera Eye sections in the other two novels. Those in *1919* parallel Dos Passos' experi- ences of war and differ very little from the passages in his war novels and in his autobiography. They are not soapbox oratory against war—rather they are poetic epiphanies—but they do raise uncomfortable ques- tions about the waste of lives and the denial of free speech to those who dissent. Commentary on the May Day 1919 celebration in Paris is less a paean to revolu- tion than to the utopia that it promises. In *The Big Money* the emphasis is on the promise and denial of basic freedom in the United States. The speaker rumi- nates about wealth and poverty: "why not tell these men stamping in the wind that we stand on a quick- sand?"; he is ashamed of himself for dreaming and not acting; he wonders "what leverage might pry the owners loose from power and bring back (I too Walt Whitman) our storybook democracy." Protest rises to a peak with the Sacco-Vanzetti case, contrasting the fate of these immigrants in Plymouth with the original settlers, who were "kingkillers haters of oppression."

Number 50, which states "they have clubbed us off the
streets they are stronger they are rich," reaches the
anguished conclusion, "all right we are two nations."

If we ask the question, What makes a man of
gentle rearing, artistic and intellectual taste, and ab-
horrence of violence turn to the revolutionary left? the
answer has been chronicled in the Camera Eyes. We
see his development through experience of war, of
capitalistic dehumanization, and of repression of dissent. The Sacco-Vanzetti case is the catalyst which
purifies him of uncertainty and commits him to the
cause of the downtrodden and the dispossessed. The
Camera Eyes suggest, without arrogance, that this is
the path a man of good will must follow through the
iron labyrinth of the twentieth century, and they provide a standard by which to measure the twelve fictional characters who are the major exhibits of the
novel.

U.S.A. in the jargon of some critics has been
called a "collective" novel. The term is unfortunate in
its ideological implications and fails to convey the
central fact that this is a novel without a protagonist,
one in which no single life provides a center of interest
and meaning. This work exhibits multiple parallel lives
on a scale never before attempted. Its form is radial;
that is, each spoke has the same importance as the
others, all converging on a common center. If the
reader's mind could, indeed, focus on all these characters at once he would perceive that unity. But since
the experience of the novel is temporal, not spatial,
simultaneity is not possible, except in brief passages,
and the reader must keep the various characters in
suspension until he can weigh them as a group.

These fictional personages fall into three cate-

gories: the twelve exemplary characters who are given
major billing by having narrative sections bear their
names; a limited number who turn up at various
points in the work as they relate to some of the above
but for whom no substantial background is provided;
and incidental ones who, however prominent, relate to
only one of the major figures, fleshing out his life,
acting as foils on occasion, but in themselves not under
examination for their own sake.

The way the narratives of the twelve major characters are woven into the novel is varied, though they
can be counted on not to appear as a block. The story
of Mac, the first one we meet, is told in seven episodes
uninterrupted by other narratives. Then three other
characters appear and 167 pages later there is a final
Mac section, after which he disappears from the novel.
Janey Williams, J. Ward Moorehouse, and Eleanor
Stoddard have name sections only in the first novel,
though they reappear in the other two. In *1919*, five
characters have name sections, three of them completely new. Two of them appear only in this volume.
Joe Williams' career comes to an end in a barroom
brawl; Daughter dies in an airplane accident. The
other, Dick Savage, continues to be important in *The
Big Money* along with Charley Anderson, who appeared in the first but not the second novel. Finally, in
The Big Money two characters, Mary French and
Margo Dowling, occupy much of the narrative. This
lack of pattern lends an air of random verisimilitude,
though with the exception of Mac all twelve are inter-
connected and nine of them do proceed to the end.

It is important to note that when name sections
for a given character cease, he is not necessarily down-
graded. J. Ward Moorehouse and Janey Williams are

ubiquitous in *1919*. Eleanor Stoddard and Eveline Hutchins are in view through all three novels. Ben Compton, who has only one name section (in *1919*), is occasionally on scene in the following work. Sometimes the same events are told from two points of view, especially in the case of Janey and Joe Williams and of Eleanor Stoddard and Eveline Hutchins. Sometimes the interconnections of the major figures seem forced, and indeed unnecessary. Nothing is gained by having Mac encounter J. Ward Moorehouse (and George H. Barrow, a continuing secondary character) in Mexico. It is amusing but of no importance that Joe Williams is the sailor whom Savage and his friends meet in a bar outside of Genoa. At the very end there is irritating contrivance when at Eveline Hutchins' party Mary French, Margo Dowling, Dick Savage, and G. H. Barrow are all brought under the same roof. Indeed if one is to fault Dos Passos' handling of the intricate counterpoint of so many lives it is in respect to the unnecessary tightness of relationships, which casts doubt on the randomness of his sampling.

The actual narrative, while more conventional than the other dimensions of the novel, does not lack technical interest. In comparison with *Manhattan Transfer*, *U.S.A.* makes very little use of dialogue and dramatic scene. What gives the various life histories impact is the use of summary stream of consciousness in language appropriate to the character. Within the limits permitted, Janey Williams or Dick Savage or Mary French comes alive because we are aware of how each perceives experience through the very language he uses. This may degenerate into formula: Eveline Hutchins' catchphrase "It's all so tiresome;" but usually the language is flexible, employing slang, profanity, simple or mannered vocabulary as they are appropriate. Because of Dos Passos' acute ear for nuances of speech, language is a refined instrument of characterization. We hear his people better than we see them, and we hear them not only in regular dialogue but in so-called narrative passages as well.

When we consider whether this cast of characters is representative, we must concede at once that it does not present an adequate cross section and that the selection is clearly and deliberately slanted in the direction of vacuity and failure. These lives may be exemplary, but most readers agree that they are exemplary of only one aspect of human endeavor. The very fact that these are hollow men and women whose course is downward constitutes an inescapable indictment of American life and institutions in their time.

If we apply criteria for success and failure in simplified terms, we must see Mac as a radical who settles complacently into the comfort of middle-class existence, Joe Williams a working stiff incapable of living beyond the moment, Janey Williams a person who achieves identity only in symbiotic relationship with the boss, Daughter an unruly youngster who flees responsibility, and Margo Dowling the synthetic product of a synthetic industry. Ben Compton exists more as horrible example, a pathetic and feckless victim of the repressive forces of society as he goes off to a twenty-year prison term at the age of twenty-two. Five of the remaining six fail even more egregiously: J. Ward Moorehouse peddling words as a public relations expert and selling himself with words as empty as his own character; Eleanor Stoddard taking refuge in a sterile elegance; Eveline Hutchins, a pursuer of pleasure who finds it all so boring that she commits

suicide; Charley Anderson, a simple man who is good
with engines but is destroyed by high living and high
finance; Dick Savage, potentially a man of sensibility,
who pursues the main chance and loses his own soul.
Only Mary French, who has genuine compassion for
the underdog, plods resolutely ahead to a worthy goal.
She will not reach it because she has no defense
against being used by others, but we admire her for
her ability to subordinate herself to the needs of
others.

These major characters nearly all come from
homes that are in some way broken, without normal
security and love, and none of them is capable of
achieving a satisfactory marital existence. Over and
over we see sex drives as a source of exploitation and
enslavement. The two working stiffs, Mac and Joe, are
trapped by nice girls who use sex first as a means to
marriage, then as coercion to insure a materially safe
existence. Janey sublimates sex in adoration of J. Ward
Moorehouse. Eleanor Stoddard, a potential lesbian,
has an occasional meaningless affair. Eveline Hutchins
sleeps around, marries Paul Johnson and soon divorces
him. Daughter is seduced by the sexually ambivalent
Dick Savage, who refuses to marry her when she becomes pregnant. Mary French accepts the free-love
doctrines of her radical friends and is let down by Don
Stevens, her communist lover. Whoring comes natu-
rally to Margo Dowling; she uses her body first to
escape poverty, then to rise to stardom. J. Ward
Moorehouse enters into two marriages for money,
sleeps with Eleanor Stoddard and Eveline Hutchins,
and is happiest submitting to the ministrations of call
girls. Charley Anderson can leave neither women nor
booze alone and is taken for all he has by his calculat-

ing wife in Bloomfield Hills, as he would have been a second time by Margo Dowling if he had lived. Dick Savage sleeps with girls without much enthusiasm; at the end we see him prey to blackmailing homosexuals in Harlem. For these people sex is Robert Penn Warren's "great twitch" with a vengeance and a major strand of the determinism of the novel. Their unsatisfactory sexual lives are damning evidence of a basic sterility in human relations.

Another curious limitation of the group chosen is what we may call a vocational inertia. They are all untrained (except Janey Williams) and drift into jobs rather than coming to adulthood with definite purpose. To be sure, Dick Savage finishes Harvard, emerging as a promising minor poet, vintage 1915, and Mary French has a couple of years at Vassar before she drops out, while Eveline Hutchins and Eleanor Stoddard have desultory interludes at the Chicago Art Institute. It must be admitted that Moorehouse teaches himself French and that Joe Williams studies to get a succession of licenses. Even though lack of advanced schooling is the norm for the generation Dos Passos is portraying, these people strike us as undisciplined, opportunistic, and drifting. A more representative cross section would show some people at least setting up and achieving goals, using their minds in a disciplined way and subordinating their egos to the demands of some profession.

Still another aspect of their lives, so prominent as to constitute a major theme, is an ineradicable inhumanity, an intolerance toward people and ideas in any way offbeat. There is snide disparagement of all who do not belong to the category of nice people. Pejorative terms like "bohunk," "guinea," "shine," "greaser," and the host of others vulgarly used to refer to the non-white Anglo-Saxons are always on the lips of Dos Passos' characters. This is but one of the ways in which he accurately, and painfully, records the speech of the people. There are more developed instances of discriminatory attitude and action. Even Mary French is disturbed because her friend Ada Cohen is so Jewish. Margo Dowling takes pleasure in humiliating her Cuban husband by making him wear a uniform and act as her chauffeur. This class- and race-consciousness separates officers from men, manual workers from white-collar workers, "muckers" of any stamp from the distinguished people in the roto-gravure section.

When the chips are down, this automatic consigning of aliens and oddballs to coventry leads to exploitation and violence. Since such people have been tagged as less than human, they are fair game. If a man is a Wobbly, he may legitimately be beaten, castrated, crucified. It is this denial of freedom of speech and action that Dos Passos returns to again and again. He can make fun of social snobbery—witness Eveline Hutchins' party for refugee Russian noblemen; what he cannot abide is persecution of dissenters. The stories of Mac, of Ben Compton, of Joe Williams, of Mary French, and of Charley Anderson in his early years are central to this theme. It is significant that Mac begins and Mary ends the novel. Mac as a boy is arrested for distributing union handbills during a strike; his uncle, a socialist, is bankrupted. Mary at the end is steadfastly trying to break down barriers, pathetically trying to convince her capitalist stepfather that the striking Appalachian miners are human beings. The three novels use the full gamut of their tech-

niques to emphasize this theme. We see a man being
run in in San Francisco for reading the Declaration of
Independence to a crowd. We are present with Ben
Compton at a riot in Everett, Washington. We are told
of the hounding of Thorstein Veblen. The examples are
legion. The weakest part of this is the attempt to show
in Ben Compton how a revolutionary is made. The
lack of psychological depth characteristic of Dos
Passos' people is fatal here. It is not enough to see Ben
pushed and broken by external forces. We need to feel
the generation of internal resolution and an anguished
perception that the system is out of joint. The inter-
larded quotations from Marx that attend Ben's development are not enough, unless indeed the author is
already being ironic about the claims of socialist doctrine.

Parallel to the theme of repression of dissent is a
second theme, the aggressive and soulless power of
wealth. This, as we have already seen, is carried chiefly
by the Newsreels and the short biographies. In the
narrative proper there are sinister background figures,
like a man named Rasmussen, who is present at the
Paris peace conference to guard the interests of Standard Oil. The war itself is repeatedly presented as an
effort to safeguard the Morgan loans to the Allies.
Since of the major figures only J. Ward Moorehouse
represents big business—and that in a parasitic way—
this part of the novel's statement is weak, suggestive
rather than convincingly documentary.

There is a unified progression of ideas as we move
through the three parts of *U.S.A.* The first presents a
fairly kindly, innocent America, where the ordinary
man's aspirations are usually blocked but where he can
dream of controlling his own destiny and throwing off

the shackles which he feels but does not analyze. The war brings an end to innocence. It is in part a diversionary action to stifle dissent at home. President Wilson becomes the villain of the piece: *1919* is an ironic contrast between the idealistic promises he made to make the world safe for democracy and the actualities of power politics as they are revealed at the peace conference. The third novel shows the fruits of this deception, of the moral and social debacle that the war is seen to have brought. The opportunities for the average man narrow. As he resists, coercion is more and more overt. The hysteria of war years becomes an habitual state of mind directed at exaggerated or imaginary dangers. The Sacco-Vanzetti case is used as the prime example, but the final scenes showing the destitution of the miners and their harsh repression by the police and courts are actually more effective. As Archibald MacLeish wrote, "America was promises." *U.S.A.* is a chronicle of promises betrayed or forgotten, of a diminution of human dignity and liberty, of a basic disregard for human worth.

The overall statement is a pessimistic one. The "American Century" proudly announced in the opening Newsreel turns out to be a fatal misadventure. The swelling imperial theme of the opening leads to military adventures in Mexico and on a grand scale in Europe, where a tremendous expenditure of blood and treasure made the world safe—for international oil. The whole of American might was turned against the aspirations of the common man as expressed in the Mexican and Russian revolutions and the abortive attempts at revolution in war-torn Europe. The novel does not examine the implications of those revolutions; it takes them on trust as consonant with the traditional

American belief in freedom. Thus abroad as well as at home, the American dream has become a nightmare.

U.S.A. is not a depression novel. It lacks the shrill immediacy and ideological confusion of such works as Jack Conroy's *The Disinherited* or Robert Cantwell's *The Land of Plenty*. But it was written during the depression, and the mounting anguish of the last volume certainly derives from the author's awareness of the havoc that a third of a century of misdirection has wrought. The reader, moreover, can supply his own scenario of economic and social decay, breadlines, foreclosures, evictions, and riots as they flow from the breakdown of the system. It was inevitable that Dos Passos should become the darling of the left during those years. None of the adherents of the socialist or communist parties could write with anything like his power. None of them grasped the fatal perspective of history, even though they were provided with a ready-made perspective by Marx. Because Dos Passos shared their passion, they allowed themselves to believe that he shared their formula for the eradication of the evils that aroused their passion. They needed his eloquence to communicate their cause. As it turned out, he was forced by his integrity to a decision that he did not need them. Theirs was, in his opinion, a tunnel vision; his compassion had a much wider temporal and spatial sweep.

This disavowal of left-wing orthodoxy is already evident in *The Big Money*. Mary French, the embodiment of radical aspiration, explicitly states that she is not a member of the Communist Party. There is enough evidence of a narrowing concern for humanity on the part of the Russian regime supplied by the Newsreels to enable us to evaluate Don Stevens' opportunism for what it is and to see Ben Compton's expulsion from the Party as a portent of its oppressive practices. Both sides are hardening. The future of genuine freedom is dark because it is threatened from left and right. The novel is in fact even more pessimistic than its critical acclaimers were willing to perceive.

5

"*. . . and Revisions*"

After *U.S.A.* Dos Passos wrote eight more novels. Three of them, *Chosen Country* (1951), *Most Likely to Succeed* (1954), and *The Great Days* (1958), have chiefly a biographical interest, indirectly reflecting certain aspects of the author's experience but telling us very little about the development of his thought. The other five are serious, if not always successful, works, continuing into the second third of the century the social chronicle that is the substance of the great trilogy.

One thing that strikes us in these later works, which the originality* and technical virtuosity of the earlier ones caused many to overlook, is that Dos Passos is not a novelist of the traditional kind. That is, he is not capable of creating a fictive world that is self-subsistent or of creating characters who are interesting in their own right by reason of their rich and varied humanity. What we come to recognize, if it is not already apparent, is that he is a writer of exemplary tales which, under the guise of fiction, analyze, comment on, and increasingly lambaste developments in American society. There are two things about these later novels that dampen the reader's enthusiasm. There is little that is new in technique to arouse interest, and the heat of a consuming idealism that sustains the chronicle of failure in *U.S.A.* gives way to an almost weary arraignment of one malfunction after another in contemporary life. From an ideological point of view Dos Passos has had second—and third—thoughts about the aspirations of the liberal left and is disenchanted with all programs for social regeneration, making on them a comprehensive assault for the falsity of their rhetoric and their corrupt pursuit of power as an end in itself.

Though the three novels *Adventures of a Young Man* (1939), *Number One* (1943), and *The Grand Design* (1949) are grouped together as a trilogy under the covering title *District of Columbia*, they have none of the cohesiveness or concentrated impact of *U.S.A.* They are loosely linked by the presence of members of the Spotswood family in all of them. Glenn, a radical and idealist who is expelled from the Communist Party and sent to his death by Party order in the Spanish Civil War, is the protagonist of the first novel. His brother Tyler, an opportunist who is the faithful lieutenant of and ultimately fall guy for a Huey Long type of politician, has a major role in the second; and their father Herbert, a sentimental idealist turned newscaster-warmonger, is central to the third. Tyler, released from prison, staggers drunkenly in and out of the last novel, and Glenn, posthumously and with heavy-handed irony, becomes a communist saint and martyr. In addition certain radical personalities from *Adventures of a Young Man* and certain predatory figures from *Number One* are carried over into *The Grand Design*, though in secondary roles. There is no innate necessity for this. Completely new casts of characters would have done as well, but the author seems intent on binding together another trilogy. It is, however, no more than three separate narratives occupying the time span from the onset of the depression to American entry into World War II. Each novel is a study of the failure of idealism in a different public context.

The scenario for *Adventures of a Young Man* is provided by the six poetic meditations which precede each chapter and end the novel. The speaker, brooding over the time of trials that the twentieth century has become for every man, laments that the American people have entered this period "with very little preparation," and have forgotten "the plain aims and purposes" for which they founded a republic. Under Wilson's leadership they both forgot Washington's advice about foreign entanglements and failed in their attempt to make the world safe for democracy, though they did learn military logistics. That war accelerated the process by which capitalism has come to exert "direct daily power over many men."

With the Russian revolution "a sizeable minority of Americans began to transfer to the Russian experiment the hopes they were heir to from the early enthusiasts for an order where men should be equal and freedom and abundance should reign." This aspiration was betrayed, for the communist regime turned out to be merely a different board of directors, one which came to exercise total power "to kill, to starve, to torture, to work without pay the suffering masses of men," breaking their wills to obedience through terror. All the devices that had been used down through the centuries to control men's minds were seized upon by the Communist Party "to serve a simple globecircling dogma: those who would not submit their will to the will of the Party . . . were enemies of the human race."

Americans, forgetting their basic ideals, were easily taken in by this propaganda, which caused them to forget that "the freedom of one class of people cannot be gained at the expense of the enslavement of another, and that means are more important than ends, because means mould institutions which frame ways of behaving, while ends are never in any man's lifetime attained."

The life and death of Glenn Spotswood are con-
firmation of this tedious poetic statement. Glenn is
young and naive, as America is young and naive, in his
understanding of social process. His heritage is a diffuse religious idealism. As counselors at a summer
camp for rich boys, he and his friend Paul Graves take
a stand against privilege and injustice and are fired.
He works his way through college, is exposed to the
writings of Henry George and other native dissidents,
has a summer experience as an itinerant worker during
which he drinks in leftwing ideas, transfers to Columbia and is drawn into radical bohemian circles, is seduced by Gladys Funaroff, a stereotyped Jewish radical to whom he represents "the confused ignorant
masses of America." Dominated by cliches, such as
"only the revolutionary working class, following in the
lead of the Russian working class, can really give us
world peace," he compromises his ideals by taking a
job in a Texas bank. In that community he encounters
and tries to do something about exploitation of Mexican workers, and is run out of town by the Ku Klux
Klan. In New York he takes the name of Crockett,
joins the Communist Party, and goes off to organize
the Appalachian miners.

From this point on there is conflict between his
humanitarian ideals and the veering, opportunistic
tactics of the Party. He reaches the point where he
refuses to be used and is expelled from the Party. He
runs into his friend Paul Graves, just back from Russia,
who has seen the way the future works and does not
like it. Then, caught up in the cause of the Spanish
Republic, he enlists as a volunteer. In Spain he immediately runs up against communist power tactics.
His Texas friend Frankie Perez tells him that they

have to fight both Franco and Moscow in order to
protect the revolution. New York communists stir up
suspicion against him. He is imprisoned on a charge of
counterrevolutionary activity, and is sent on a suicide
mission to the front lines, where he is killed.

Thus described, Glenn Spotswood is very much a
stereotype, and we cannot get around the fact that he is
a wooden and unconvincing figure. He exists to demonstrate the difference between genuine radical idealism
and cynical communist exploitation of that idealism.
We never know how he thinks or how he feels as an
individual. He has no substance except for what is
useful for his role as fall guy in the arena of radical
politics. His development as a radical is too mechanical, his ruthless destruction by the communist hier-
archy is too perfunctory. The whole novel is obviously
controlled by polemic purpose. The only times it
comes alive are in scenes among the striking coal
miners and passages describing illegal crossing into
Spain through the high Pyrenees. This experiential
freshness is in painful contrast to the formulaic conduct of the rest.

It is a bad novel, but that is not the reason its
author's reputation went into eclipse. Nothing could
have been a more deliberate flouting of the radical
establishment than his attitude toward those on the
side of the loyalist government. The passion this conflict aroused on the left all over the world may not
have been out of proportion to its importance, but that
passion precluded any objective examination of the
situation in Spain. To state that the war was less than
a watershed in human history, or that the stream of
history was equally roiled on either side of the watershed, was to break faith with radical orthodoxy. The

kindest comment on Dos Passos' apostasy was that he
was confused. Michael Gold declared that his deser-
tion of the communist cause proved that he hated the
whole human race.

Number One, by contrast, is extraordinarily well
done. In part this is because it is less programmed and
is almost out of time. It is a simple and deadly demonstration of the corruptness of power with minimal attention to broad social chronicle. This is not a new
subject in American fiction, but Dos Passos' treatment
deserves to stand in the front rank between Robert
Herrick's *The Memoirs of an American Citizen*, which
preceded it by nearly forty years, and Robert Penn
Warren's *All the King's Men*, which came out a few
years after *Number One*.

The object of examination and attack is a radical
reformer demagogue. It is obvious that Huey Long
served as model for the fictional Chuck Crawford, but
it is Huey Long as generic example, not as a specific
individual. There is a fatal gap between the stirring
words of the politician on the make and the venal
actuality of the way he gets and uses power.

The novel dips into Crawford's life at five reveal-
ing episodes in his career. We see him first as a simple
congressman trying to get enough news coverage to
build himself up for the Senate. He sets a little trap to
get his picture taken with a powerful senator, then
apologizes: "You got to forgive ole Chuck. He don't
mean no harm." After this exercise in disingenuousness
he goes for a night on the town. When he learns next
morning that the incumbent senator has died, he decides to run for his seat. The second episode, some
months later, is a day on the campaign trail during
which he manages to bring a standoffish governor to

heel. In a similar scene later on he succeeds in getting his delegation seated at the national Democratic convention, thereby consolidating his control of state patronage and laying the foundation for a try at the presidency.

These three instances of political charisma and guile are balanced by two scenes in which the man of the people mulcts the people. He sets up an elaborate illegal deal in which, as he says repeatedly, he is "as clean as a hound's tooth," by which he means that there is no way of his being caught. The scheme consists of getting the Utilities Commission, which he controls, to lease certain oil-bearing state lands to a dummy corporation which will front for him. He justifies this on the grounds that as a result the wells will be sunk and the people of this great state will share in the royalties: "The rest of it's technicalities . . . I'll be merely an employee of this corporation as I am of the sovereign people. . . . This thing's as clean as a hound's tooth." The crowning touch in this finagling is that signatures are notarized by an ex-felon in a nightclub where Crawford is preoccupied with satisfying the demands of a call girl.

The final incident occurs after Crawford's enemies in the state and national administrations succeed in breaking the swindle wide open. He throws his devoted lieutenant Tyler Spotswood to the wolves and gets off scot-free. As Tyler has already observed, "He hasn't a thought in the world except for himself."

All these scenes are brilliantly realized in dialogue. Crawford's is the dominant voice; by his words he shows himself up as the hollow, venal, crafty man he is. The narrator disappears entirely; by no shade of emphasis does he pass judgment. Nor is there much

comment or moralizing by fictional characters. There
is no need. We see the corrupt well-being that Crawford achieves. We see those whom he corrupts or de-
feats. His wife leaves him. Tyler Spotswood destroys
himself in his service. He is "housebroken," as Crawford condescendingly observes, a safe man to take care
of his wife Sue Ann, a safe man to pimp for him, a safe
man to bribe and cajole and lie for him, a safe man
finally to take the rap. Hearing Crawford on the radio
declaring that he has been "betrayed by false friends,"
Tyler with unexpected insight bursts out:

"Well, he's a goddam liar. . . . We can't sell out on the
people, but the trouble is that me, I'm just as much the
people as you or any other son of a bitch. If we want to
straighten the people out we've got to start with number
one, not that big wind. . . . You know what I mean. I got
to straighten myself out first, see."

The poetic interludes in this novel are used to
bring rhetoric down to earth by asking what the concrete referents of glowing empty words really are. This
note is struck in the first sentence: "When you try to
find the people, always in the end it comes down to
somebody, somebody working maybe," a man on a
harrow with a pair of mules and his wife hanging out
the wash and his kid with the whooping cough, or "a
middleaged mechanic setting a bearing in the back of
a concrete garage," or a boy of seventeen, a radio ham,
aspiring to the universe but weighed down by "the
cramped restriction of every day, the worn soles of his
shoes, the frayed trouser cuff, the spots on his only
good necktie, the crazy need for change." These Whit-
manesque passages are by no means merely a senti-

mental hymn to the common man. They are a warning to him to preserve his independence and individuality, not to be conned or mesmerized into the mass man whom the spellbinding politician wants to subdue to his use, and to ignore or discard when he is through with him. The demagogue's use of *the people* is meaningless, but the people exist, as individuals, and as individuals they must forge their own destiny, not leave it in the hands of the Chuck Crawfords and the Huey Longs.

The Grand Design, which completes this trilogy, is unfortunately a blurred and unsatisfactory piece of work. Like its predecessors it has as its target the arrogation of power to one man or to a self-designated group, with consequent subordination of the individual to impersonal and unresponsive authority, in this case the bureaucracy of the New Deal from its beginnings in 1933 to its gradual dismantling under the pressure of World War II. This canvas is too broad for the author to handle it with any clarity of outline. He is unable to mass detail effectively or to give his usual two-dimensional characters even minimal definition. The best he can do is to give a satiric picture of big and little Caesars, big and little Messiahs hopping ineffectually around Washington like chickens with their heads off.

Franklin Roosevelt, the one defined historical figure, receives ambivalent treatment. On the one hand, he is the confident leader who extemporizes measures to counter the depression and restore hope to the hopeless. On the other, he leads us into war, using the anticipated crisis as an excuse to break with tradition and run for a third term. He allows the immediate necessities of war to undermine the long-range and

valid goals of the New Deal. The next to the last inter-
chapter meditation on history charges that "By the
modulations of his voice into the microphone he
played on the American people. We danced to his
tune. Third term. Fourth term. Indispensable. War is a
time of Caesars." He and the other wartime dictators
"without consulting their constituents, revamped geog-
raphy, divided up the bloody globe and let the free-
doms out. And the American people were supposed to
say thank you for the century of the Common Man
turned over for relocation behind barbed wire so help
him God." The charge is summed up in these terms:
We learned how to win the war, "but we have not
learned, in spite of the Constitution and the Declaration of Independence and the great debates at Rich-
mond and Philadelphia how to put power over the
lives of men into the hands of one man and to make
him use it wisely."

However, the focus is not on Roosevelt's arrogation of power, which, rightly or wrongly, would provide a clear and straightforward argument. It is a
much vaguer subject, centralization of power in Washington, a city which on the first page is described as
having "colonnades that echoed Rome." Twice during
the Roosevelt years hordes of bureaucrats descended
on the capital: "Some represented everybody, some
represented nobody, themselves maybe. They spoke
for us. They were professionals: lawyers, laborleaders,
sociologists, economics professors fresh from the class-
room, analysts, publicists, officers of foundations and
learned societies, merchandisers, brokers, experts in
this and in that, big names to set up on the letterheads
of committees."

The first wave were the do-gooders of the New

Deal; the second were the managers of the war effort.
Each group—and often it was the same individuals
doubling in brass—succumbed to the occupational disease of the capital: intrigue, power politics, jockeying
for position, building personal empires. Like Jed Far-
rington in *Adventures of a Young Man*, they found it a
fascinating game of chess, where human beings were
nothing but pawns.

There is a temptation to read this novel as a
roman à clef about the Roosevelt years. Fortunately,
thanks in part to the law of libel, that is not possible.
Certainly the Secretary of Agriculture, Walker Watson, will call Henry Wallace to mind, but he also has
attributes of Harry Hopkins. Because of their role in
government, other fictional characters bear some re-
semblance to Milo Perkins, Jesse Jones, and Mr. Justice Frankfurter. But derisory as the treatment of Watson is, it is not Henry Wallace who is being pilloried,
but a functionary who is a composite, an invention.
The same is true of other suggested actual figures.
Weak as it is in certain respects, the novel is better
than that. It is not out to get certain real people but
seeks to illuminate a general truth about a time when
those figures did indeed play a part.

There are three principal characters: Millard Carroll, who comes from the Southwest to head an important agency in the Department of Agriculture; Paul
Graves (from the earlier novel), a scientist who is
interested in developing superior strains of farm prod-
ucts and in fostering the family farm; and Walker
Watson, a do-gooder who loses his direction in the
maze of political life and who by indecision and personal ambition impedes what those under him are trying to do. The novel ends when Carroll and Graves

can stand their frustration no longer and resign. Surrounding these men is a host of minor characters, many of them drawn from the preceding parts of the trilogy, who join the New Deal or the war effort to forward their own careers or to implement their beliefs. They veer with the wind, especially the communists, who oppose preparation for war until Russia is attacked; a notable trimmer is Herbert Spotswood, an old antiwar man and former functionary of the League of Nations, who now uses his radio broadcasts to whip up war sentiment.

The liveliest part of the narrative is that which follows the career of Paul Graves. He is an engaging figure, partly because he has already been established as a personality, partly because—something rare with Dos Passos—he has unexpected dimensions. He never adapts to Washington. He is happiest on his trips into the field, that is, to the farm belt, where he has a habit of meeting untamed individualists and drawing them out. He comes to believe that help and control from Washington are humiliating and self-defeating, robbing men of dignity and enterprise. He fails in his effort to stem the amassing of bureaucratic power. He concludes that it is less a matter of the old saw that power corrupts and absolute power corrupts absolutely than it is that power voraciously feeds on itself and expands geometrically, not arithmetically, a Malthusian law for politics.

The novel is not clear about what can be done to oppose this concentration, given the fact that something has to be done to pull the country out of the depression and that modern war does demand the full mobilization of resources under what amounts to dictatorship. The concluding words seem to be a hopeless plea in the face of the actual demands of the time:

The republic's foundations are not in the sound of words, they are in the shape of our lives, fellow citizens. They trace the outlines of a grand design. To achieve greatness a people must have a design before them too great for accomplishment. Some things we have learned, but not enough; there is more to learn. Today we must learn to found again in freedom our republic.

Dos Passos' next fictional volley at the coercive force of bigness came eleven years after the second trilogy. *Midcentury* (1960), which he described as being in the modified manner of *U.S.A.*, is impressive for its technical originality and for the incisiveness of its statement, even though that statement is one-sided. It gave no comfort to the author's former associates and admirers since it is an attack on labor unions. When we consider that in *U.S.A.* those who devoted their lives to unionization were among the author's heroes, this attack represents an even more dramatic turnabout than his repudiation of the Communist Party and the New Deal. It is as though he has now gone back on the last article in his liberal creed.

In this work the narrative is supported by various kinds of document. There are twenty-five "Documentaries," equivalent to the Newsreels of the earlier work. There are seven "Investigator's Notes," pseudo-transcripts of secret testimony about union tyranny and terror. The Camera Eye is not revived, tacit admission perhaps that poetic insight has had to give way to the dulling impact of reality.

But the short biography appears again, less objec-

tive even than before, clearly manipulated to make a
point. The imperial theme which had bothered Dos
Passos from the beginning sounds again in his portrait
of Douglas MacArthur, "Pronconsul" in the Far East
who had to be cut down to size. The next two
sketches, "Analyst" (Freud) and "The Promised Land
(New Style)" (Harry Bridges), provide a devastating
double-barreled attack on ideologies: "These are the
brainwashers, the twin myths of Marx and Freud,"
two illusory promises of secular salvation. A clutch of
labor leaders, Tobin, Beck, and Hoffa, receives caustic
treatment; the attitude toward that old warrior John
L. Lewis is ambivalent. Walter Reuther appears in a
generally favorable light. He is a successor to Debs,
and "a vote for Debs was a vote for man's perfectibility," but the authorial voice now seems to hesitate over
the possibility of perfectibility.

Among the other biographies there is a fairly wide
gamut of acceptance and debunking. Eleanor Roosevelt, "Rover," gets sardonic tribute: "First Lady of the
United Nations; uplift become global." Robert Oppenheimer, the physicist, who was crucified by power-
hungry politicians, is at once martyr and portent as he
faces "The difficulty of discovering where the cleavage
lies (not outside but inside civilization) between the
powers that would destroy and the powers that would
save the spirit of man. . . ."

Some insight into those powers comes in the final
pair of biographies—General William F. Dean, who
was held captive by the North Koreans for three years,
and James Dean, the movie star, who was killed in an
automobile accident at twenty-four. The pairing of
these two men provides a crashing climax to the novel
in its contrast of value systems. The General, subjected

to pressure and torture, never gave in to his captors; his quiet heroism arose from his knowing who he was and where he belonged in the scheme of things. Many of his men, however, surrendered and later defected to communism because "Nobody had ever told them anything except to get more and do less. . . . The Communist indoctrinators were able to appeal to a sort of ignorant idealism that is the dead shell of the protestant ethic our fathers lived by."

James Dean goes a step further than they, embodying the ultimate break with the former value system. There is no dead shell left, only a shallow egotism, a posturing before the mirror of the adulatory young, "the lost cats in love with themselves just like James Dean."

This concluding judgment about America in mid-century is an extrapolation beyond the evidence of the novel, which, weighted as it is, does not support so sweeping a statement. It rests rather on the paradox enunciated in the case of Oppenheimer: man in the space age reaches for the stars with some assurance of reaching them, yet he is still a jungle creature in his relations with his fellows and in his use of institutions. This contrast between aspiration and human imperfection—violence, vulgarity, not to mention venery—is the constant burden of the twenty-five Documentaries, is the substance of the Investigator's Notes, and pervades the fictional narratives.

In this novel the narrative strands are much reduced in number from what they were in *U.S.A.* The most extended, that of Blackie Bowman, who recounts his life as he lies dying in a Veterans' Hospital, recalls the lives of Mac, Joe, and Ben in the earlier work as it summarizes the odds against the ordinary working stiff through the whole course of the century. It expresses once more the naive expectations of pre-communist radical movements and shows something of the hardened dogma of those who support the Party. Blackie Bowman, needing help, could not find it in any kind of ideology, nor could he find it in himself. The second narrative presents two veterans of World War II, Terry Bryant and Frank Worthington, union men from way back who throw themselves into unionization of the rubber industry in the years after the war. They are shocked at the power tactics of the unions but get nowhere in their attempt to fight and expose it. Worthington is moved upstairs, where he does not know what is going on; Bryant is kicked out of the union and becomes a taxi driver in the hope that he can make an honest living as an independent man. This part of the novel is closely paralleled by the case histories of the Investigator's Notes, which give the impression of being a selection of the most lurid testimony gathered by the McClellan Committee. Finally there is the story of Jasper Milliron (as a young man he appeared as one of the background figures in *Chosen Country*). His experience of corporate infighting differs only in superficial politeness from what goes on in the unions. He too is pushed out, but with a cushion of wealth to fall on. The various narrative strands converge when he backs his son-in-law and Terry Bryant in their effort to establish their taxi business against the resistance of a corrupt monopoly. They win, but Terry Bryant is killed in that war.

What this convergence of narratives establishes is that power-seeking business and power-seeking unions are indistinguishable, each, in the classic phrase, saying "The public be damned." In each case violence and skulduggery are the rule. In each case there is jungle warfare, and when a man loses the fight he is through. There is no place in the system for the independent man.

During the years in which he was writing his last novel Dos Passos referred to it as "The Thirteenth Chronicle," calling it on one occasion "a last forlorn Chronicle of Despair." His publishers have appropriately retitled it *Century's Ebb*, as it depicts a further subsidence of American life during the years from the death of Malcolm X to the launching of Apollo 10.

In this work short biographies or profiles provide the major nonnarrative material. The first of these is of Walt Whitman, a distinct departure, since he had previously invoked only contemporary figures. One of the best and most admiring is of George Orwell. But as in previous novels they are more often used to condemn than to praise and here they are more often directed at personalities on the left than at those on the right. As usual there are several fictional strands, of which Jay Pignatelli provides the central one. The main targets are again the dehumanizing effects of authoritarianism and bureaucracy, that is, the monolithic state. The author's concern has not diminished and neither have the available examples. There is no change in his pessimistic view of the state of the nation. Throughout he uses Whitman as a kind of touchstone, a fellow analyst of the chances of democracy. At the beginning of Part II a quotation from *Democratic Vistas* both recalls Whitman's misgivings and serves to sum up Dos Passos' contemporary despair:

I will not gloss over the appalling dangers of universal suffrage . . . the battle, advancing, retreating, between

democracy's convictions, aspirations and the people's crude-
ness, vice, caprices . . . with unprecedented material ad-
vancement—society in these States is canker'd, crude,
superstitious, rotten. . . . Never was there more hollowness
of heart . . . the underlying principles of the States not
generally believed in . . . Coming down to what is of the
only real importance, Personalities, and examining mi-
nutely, we question, we ask: Are these indeed men worthy
of the name?

6

~~~~~~

Incorruptible Witness

Throughout his life Dos Passos the novelist also had a parallel vocation as observer, analyst, and philosopher of social institutions. For thirty years this interest was subordinate to and supportive of his fiction. For the last twenty years the relationship was reversed. Fiction mirroring contemporary life yielded place to reflections about it and a search for permanent values by which to judge it, values which he found blazoned in the history of the first decades of the republic. An inductive approach to the contemporary scene gave way to a deductive speculation about what makes a good society. As the writer became more and more disaffected with the present he turned to the past for guidance and comfort.

He was to the end a reporter with an almost obsessive desire to see and to set down what he saw, with a confident reliance on his own senses and his own judgment. We have seen that his early travels were dominated by a normal youthful desire to experience the exotic, to immerse himself in new sights and sounds and smells. Then at a certain point he embarked on a voyage of discovery of American society; the fruits of that journey, largely of the mind, are his major novels. What is less immediately apparent is that during those years he was also making a comprehensive assessment of the social and political revolutions of the twentieth century. It was not merely his own country that he judged and found wanting. His most vitriolic commentary he directed at the Soviet Union and its socialist fellow travelers. Decades before Aleksandr Solzhenitsyn appeared on scene, he discerned and inveighed against the tyrannies which the latter has documented in *The Gulag Archipelago*. However much of a troglodyte Dos Passos may have sounded in some of his later utterances about society, by his stubborn and independent witness against the Soviet Union he performed an important service in keeping the record straight.

When he proclaimed himself a socialist during the war years and uttered intemperate eulogies of revolution, he was indulging in legitimate youthful enthusiasm. After all, in that dawn it was bliss to be alive and to look forward to a sweeping and immediate redressing of all past injustices and exploitation. But even then he had the saving grace of skepticism. As early as 1919, after a look at the new republican regime in Portugal, he commented that he was more impressed by early Portuguese painting than he was by the new government: "I found the politicians grandiloquent and evasive. Their air of ineffectual benevolence rubbed me the wrong way. The working people seemed unnecessarily grubby and downtrodden and illiterate." He was to make the same observations about the new Spanish republic in the early Thirties: the men in power seemed content to batten on the labor of the workers and to do little for them.

At no point was he taken in by ideologies. This was a major point of contention between him and his doctrinaire colleagues in the New Playwrights' Theatre; he had no interest in making a play conform to the current Party line. He concedes that "I had seceded privately [from the United States] the night Sacco and Vanzetti were executed. It was not that I had joined the communists. The more I saw of the Party the more I felt that the kind of world they wanted had nothing in common with the kind of world I wanted. I wasn't joining anybody. I seceded into my private conscience like Thoreau in Concord jail." It is interesting that during the Sacco-Vanzetti demonstrations, even keyed up as he was, he was "frightened by the tense righteousness of the faces . . . There's something threatening about the unanimity of protest"—a phenomenon that disturbed many during the student riots of the Sixties.

When we remember that the ideological ferment of the Twenties and Thirties centered on economic doctrines and programs for sharing wealth, Dos Passos' position is startlingly heterodox. At no point in his career did he deliver himself at length on economic subjects. While his novels portray industrial America and show substantial maldistribution of wealth, none of his characters has much to say in terms of theoretical economics, and such comments as there are come out in dogmatic formulations far removed from actual human participation in economic life. Dos Passos was simply not with it in respect to the prevailing winds of doctrine of those years. Instead he was consistently looking at the impact of systems of production—socialist, communist, or capitalist—on human lives, on the freedom and well-being of individuals. This is either a very old-fashioned or a very new-fashioned position. It boils down to a concern about personal liberty that harks back to the great ferment of the eighteenth century that produced both the French and American revolutions. In short, he brings to the new economic state of the twentieth century a system of values and measurement outside its professed terms of reference.

Dos Passos' one and only trip to Russia took place in 1928. After his bouts with the ideologues of the New Playwrights' Theatre he wanted to see for himself. It was a good time to go. The Russians were in a welcoming mood toward foreigners. Though Trotsky had been exiled, Stalin did not yet have absolute power. The American author was able to see more and to penetrate to more places than even official visitors who came after him. He was delighted by the people he met, by their "entrancing curiosity about everything under the sun." "I got the feeling that, in spite of the destruction of so many talents in the liquidation of the old educated and governing classes, the Great Russians still comprised one of the world's major reservoirs of brains." But he was also aware of repression, of the lurking terror not far below the surface of a police state. As he was waiting for his train to leave Russia, friends from the Sanitary Propaganda Theatre asked him to state whether he was for them or against them, wanting him "to show your face." He did not answer as he jumped on the train. "I liked and admired the Russian people. I had enjoyed their enormous and varied country, but when next morning I crossed the Polish border—Poland was not Communist then—it was like being let out of jail." When he was invited to the Second World Plenum of the International Bureau of Revolutionary Literature in Kharkov in 1930, he did not go. Nor, apparently, was he ever tempted to visit Russia again.

In September 1932, Edmund Wilson and fifty-two other artists and intellectuals published an open letter declaring their support for the Communist Party in the November presidential election. A month later they organized the League of Professional Writers for Foster and Ford (the Party candidates for President and Vice-President) and expanded their letter into a pamphlet entitled *Culture and Crisis*. Sherwood Anderson, John Dos Passos, Lincoln Steffens, and Edmund Wilson were among those signing. Just as he had cast his first vote for the socialist Debs in 1920 (more out of symbolic protest than doctrinal conviction, he said later), so in 1932 Dos Passos voted the communist ticket out of disillusionment with the major parties. (He had covered both the major party conventions for the *New Republic*, and was impressed by the promises of neither.) Yet in 1934 he was among the signers of "An Open Letter to the Communist Party" in protest against a communist breakup of a socialist meeting in Madison Square Garden. Late in that year he wrote Edmund Wilson that the Kirov trials, the harbinger of Stalin's tyrannical absolutism, had "completely destroyed my benefit-of-the-doubt attitude . . . From now on events in Russia have no more interest—except as a terrible example—for world socialism—if you take socialism to mean the educative or constructive tendency rather than politics." Within a few weeks he was writing Wilson again to declare his repudiation of any of the Marxist parties—"the whole thing has entered the realm of metaphysical and religious discussion." The "new terror" in Russia, he says, or hopes, is alienating workers everywhere. If it came to a choice, he would prefer the despotism of Henry Ford, the United Fruit and the Standard Oil, to that of Earl Browder and company. It is his conclusion that "some entirely new attack on the problem of human freedom under monopolized industry has got to be worked out."

In a critique, "The Failure of Marxism," published twenty years later, Dos Passos comments that the "liberal" vocabulary has become a definite hindrance to understanding the world since World War II. (He earlier charged that the "virtuous aura" of socialist vocabulary implanted in the "confused region of the popular mind" made communist propagandizing easy. Satisfied with slogans, people showed little curiosity about how a socialist state actually works.) He contends that the contradiction is no longer between capitalism and socialism but "between the sort of organization that stimulates growth and the sort that fastens on society the dead hand of bureaucratic routine or the suckers of sterile vested interests. The road must be kept open for experiment." As he looks beyond the borders of the United States he sees the monolithic immobility of the Soviet state, which has neither expanded individual liberty nor provided a wider distribution of the good things of life. He sees the rest of the world "becoming a museum of socialist failures." Even in England (he took a special look at the Labor government after the war) there has been a contraction of personal liberty, and socialism there has "accomplished little more than to freeze the capitalist economy at its point of least efficiency." He complains in one context after another during his later years that, just as technology is making possible a really widespread well-being, "the masses of mankind, under the rule of communist dictatorships, are being plunged back into a regime of servitude such as has not existed in the West since the days of serfdom."

It is here that Dos Passos' weakness is most evident. He has no pragmatic solutions to offer, and his constant harping on the dangers of socialism-communism and the consequent plea to stick with what we have is not easily to be distinguished from a die-hard conservatism, a viewing with alarm of anything that upsets the status quo. It gets him into some odd and untenable positions, such as praising Edmund Wilson for refusing to pay his income tax. To the end of his life he remained torn between the hope inherent in American technology (he was present at Cape Canaveral for the launching of Apollo 10) and his fears that things can only get worse until they are completely immobilized by the bureaucratic government.

Perhaps sensing that he had nothing to offer for present problems but a tiresomely admonitory finger, he early sought understanding and philosophical direction in the study of history. As soon as he finished *U.S.A.* he turned to the early years of the republic, a period as full of trials as the present, but one in which right principles prevailed. After the war this study became a passion, displacing the writing of novels as his chief occupation. From the wide reading and research that occupied him for two decades there emerged four volumes of history or, more properly, historical narrative, since he brought to this form a liveliness and command of detail that are almost novelistic. The first volume, *The Head and Heart of Thomas Jefferson* (1954), is inspirational, a gathering together of writings which express Jefferson's most important ideas and aspirations. *The Men Who Made the Nation* (1957) and *The Shackles of Power* (1966) are closely packed accounts of the first fifty years of the emerging republic under the guiding genius of Jefferson. *Mr. Wilson's War* (1962) presents a counterstatement, a demonstration of where in our history basic principle was betrayed. The roles of archangel and devil assigned to these two leaders are obviously oversimplified and do violence to historical truth, but they do bring the author's political convictions into dramatic focus.

Paramount in Jefferson's thought was his belief in man's perfectibility. Through education and by the removal of institutional shackles man would have no trouble governing himself and political organization would be at a minimum. This was a widely shared view during the Enlightenment and after. If such changes were made, Saint Simon, the French social philosopher, believed that a new political era would arise in the Old World as well as the New. Jefferson was less sanguine on that point but he had the highest hopes for the United States. As he wrote John Adams late in life:

I think the best remedy is exactly that provided by all our constitutions, to leave to the citizens the free election and separation of the aristoi from the pseudo-aristoi, of the wheat from the chaff. in general they will elect the real good and wise. in some instances wealth may corrupt or birth blind them, but not in sufficient degree to endanger the society.

Dos Passos caps his eulogistic life of Jefferson with an account of the travels of Alexis de Tocqueville and Gustave de Beaumont five years after the philosopher-president's death. As aristocrats they feared the spread of democracy in France and were certainly not predisposed to praise the American experiment. Yet Tocqueville early wrote to a friend his admiration for "the ease with which they do without government." He was enchanted with Josiah Quincy's description of the United States as "a union of small republics," implying both a town-meeting type of participation and a governmental apparatus reduced to a minimum. This, as Dos Passos saw it, was the Jeffersonian ideal.

A second, and protective, article of faith of the Founding Fathers was that the republic must stay out of European affairs. Washington's admonition is well known. Jefferson delivered himself in the same terms when he wrote to President Monroe on the eve of proclamation of the Monroe Doctrine: "Our first and fundamental maxim should be, never to entangle ourselves in the broils of Europe. Our second never to suffer Europe to intermeddle with cis-Atlantic affairs." If America was to avoid the downward course of other empires, it must remove itself from the contagion endemic in those empires.

The charge Dos Passos makes against the Wilson presidency a hundred years after Jefferson is that it violated both these principles. It led us into war when we should have stayed on the sidelines, thereby permanently entangling us in the broils of Europe. It created a base of such magnitude and far-reaching power to coerce and confuse that the simple citizen was no longer able to discern and choose the aristoi rather than the pseudo-aristoi. The author labels the section dealing with going to war "The Birth of Leviathan," referring to Thomas Hobbes' conception of the repressive, monolithic leviathan state. Overnight the militia "found themselves in the straitjacket of a military caste system which ran counter to all the habits of democracy." Freedom of thought and expression were sharply curtailed: "To turn the whole nation into a team it was not enough to punish the expression of the wrong opinions. It was necessary to disseminate the right opinions." Even worse, "In lashing people up to a maximum war effort the Wilson administration unleashed blind hatreds and suspicions against foreigners and foreign ideas, and in fact against any ideas at all, that could hardly be controlled once their imagined usefulness, as a part of the psychology of total war, was at an end." This had the unfortunate consequence of turning "obstreperous and nonconformist youth" toward Soviet Russia, where they found "the righteous cause their fathers sought in following Wilson and Roosevelt and Bryan. To them the soviets were spontaneous self-governing assemblies like New England town meetings. . . ." And, of course, under Wilson government grew big: "That summer of 1917 saw the beginning of the proliferation of federal agencies that grew into the leviathan of years to come."

The character of Jefferson is of course too pure: in his time he was a consummate manipulator of men. Wilson's character and principles are too grossly blackened. Not all the evils of the rest of the century came to pass because of the presence of "that man in the White House." Dos Passos takes no account of historical or economic necessity in determining the path the nation was to follow. He prefers to see history as the product of the actions of great men, or at any rate powerful men, which in a sense is a denial of Jeffersonian principle. At no point does he attempt to come to terms with the fact that the Jeffersonian dream rests on a small, homogeneous, agricultural population. He never wrestled with the problem of numbers (210,000,000 Americans in 1970 at the time of his death), and he made insufficient recognition of the demands of a sophisticated technology, in euphoric moments only seeing its achievements as proof of the innate goodness of man. The example of the Founding Fathers may still be inspiring in the abstract, but neither Dos Passos nor anyone else is able to tell us how they would have met the problems of the present day, except, of course, with meticulous and continuing probity in the conduct of their office.

The crux of the problem is human perfectibility

and human capacity for self-determination. Jefferson and others of his philosophical persuasion believed in it. Dos Passos wanted to believe in it. Radical movements without exception assert it, whatever their deep-down beliefs. Man is a Prometheus. Freed of the shackles of custom, of ignorance, of institutions, and of semantic confusion, he will unfailingly choose what is good and right for himself and his fellows. The fire of youth is fueled by this bright expectation. It is rarely sustained, though it need not turn to suffocating ashes. But in time a Wordsworth settles down to an establishment sinecure; the student radical of the Sixties in the next decade assumes a mortgage in the suburbs and daily commutes to his job at IBM.

As novelist Dos Passos is unequivocal in what he shows about human perfectibility. He may hold the dream in his heart, but the actuality of his fiction contradicts it. There is a persistent plea that the little man, weak and defenseless, be given a better break; yet we see his major figures consistently overborne by external pressures and their own inadequacies. The only possible exception is Jay Pignatelli in *Chosen Country,* whose new-found land is the private sanctuary of marriage with Lulu Harrington. But that is a separate peace and avoids the issue (which will be revived in *Century's Ebb*).

Outside the novels he vacillates on this question. In his youth he said he could not be an anarchist because he did not have enough faith in human nature. That faith diminished under the lash of experience, especially with those professing faith. Yet human grace and cooperation under stress would sporadically cause the flame of belief to flare up brightly. On his travels around the country to observe the nation at

war in the mid-Forties, he reported enthusiastically
that "the war effort on the whole seemed to be push-
ing the country closer than it had ever been toward
our old Populist ideal of a classless society." The first
steps toward the conquest of space were another sign
of man's infinite capacity, of the actualization of a
dream. During the Sixties, he took an optimistic view
of the future and wished he were a great deal younger.
He thought that the period we were going through
(1968) was the toughest since the Civil War but on
his travels he got a good feeling of life and energy: "I
don't need to go to Australia yet." In another mood
that same year he wrote to his daughter Lucy that
"People are going to face up to the fact that there is a
great deal more evil than good in the human character
and the monster has to be kept under control." Here at
the age of seventy-two he makes categorical, if tran-
sient, denial of the hope and faith of twenty-two. We
need neither condemn nor condone. For whom after
fifty years of buffeting do things look the same?

Beyond the philosophical question of perfectibility or non-perfectibility—free will versus determinism
—there is the secular one of the durability of nations.
On his grand tour as a youngster of fifteen Dos Passos,
with a copy of *The Decline and Fall* in his hand, sat
on the Capitoline Hill and mused with Gibbon and
Henry Adams over the fall of Rome, a harmless, sentimental pose, lamenting events safely frozen in the
past. But the past is precedent, and as "the American
century" moved painfully on he saw it as ominous
portent: the American experiment might not be an
exception after all. He wanted to repudiate both Ma-
caulay's and Tocqueville's speculation that in time this
nation would rejoin the stream of history and no

longer maintain its exceptional course. In 1955, writing
to some German students to explain our uniqueness,
he concluded: "Selfgovernment, through dangers and
distortions and failures, is the American cause. Faith in
selfgovernment, when all is said and done, is faith in
the eventual goodness of man." In "Cogitations in a
Roman Theatre" (1964), not far from the Capitoline
Hill, he again broods over the lessons of the past: "For
a number of generations we thought the Declaration
of Independence had repealed history." Now we are
beginning to discern that "One of the teachings of
history is that whole nations and tribes of men can be
crushed under the imperial weight of institutions of
their own devising." Even though he goes on to say
that history also shows that "a divine something in the
human spirit" has managed to safeguard men from
destruction, his underlying fear is evident: What will
keep America from going the way of Rome? Individual destinies and national destiny are linked in his
political thought as they are in his novels. His two
vocations of novelist and observer of institutions are
ultimately one.

It is that duality that sets his work apart. Individ-
ually his novels must be read as chronicles of the
times. In their totality they chart an individual's response to those times. Decades before the Vietnam
war the antennae of the artist picked up vibrations of
disillusionment not felt by others, just as he recorded
doubts first about the hectic vanities of the Twenties
and then of the panaceas for the ills that he had de-
tected. If Dos Passos' novels continue to be read into
the twenty-first century, when the data of daily existence that he uses are already as obscure as the details
used by Elizabethan playwrights, it will not be pri-

marily because they are interesting period pieces but because they document the experience of an intelligent and sensitive man in those times. This is an illogical and perverse outcome of the attempt of the objective, impersonal narrator to refine himself out of existence. But that is the way it is: the novels are a personal record.

We must conclude that he is a chronicler, not a creator in an absolute sense. He lacks invention, preferring to draw over and over again on his own experiences to give body to the lives of his fictional characters. He never deserts the enclosed arena of observed data. He is shackled to earth, or rather to history. When he creates characters they do not take off on their own but are rigidly controlled by their function, a representative function. There is no temptation to speculate about them in other situations. There is no hint of quirks and oddities, of unexpected dimensions beyond what the demonstration demands. Of the characters in *U.S.A.* Charley Anderson alone has a vitality that suggests a fuller being; with more sustained and varied development he could have become one of those generic figures who lend their names to a whole category of human behavior, a Studs Lonigan, an Emma Bovary, a Frank Cowperwood. The rest fit comfortably in their appointed slots and stay there.

Although some critics seem to identify Dos Passos as primarily a satirist—and it is true that on occasion by accumulation of extreme cases he may produce a satiric effect—his method is not satiric but analytic. Both methods seek to instruct, but in different ways. The satirist seizes on a salient characteristic, isolates it, and by exaggeration, by overdrawing makes it ridiculous, warning his reader of its unacceptability and encouraging amendment. Dos Passos, if anything, underdraws. He leaves out complicating lines, he de-individualizes, so that the representative or exemplary nature of his exhibit will be plain. Edmund Wilson, after publication of *Adventures of a Young Man*, chided him for making it too extroverted, that is, for its simplified and strictly external portrait of the development of a radical. The author defended his "behavioristic method," saying it was one he had been trying to elaborate for many years: "By behavioristic method I mean the method of generating the insides of the characters by external description." He cites Defoe and other English novelists as practicing this method right up to the time of the romantic school, and says of his own predilection that to ask him to be less extroverted would be like asking Joyce to be less introverted. In either case the method is the artist.

Whatever its limitations, it is an old and distinguished method. The French critic Sainte-Beuve in reviewing *Madame Bovary* pointed out that Flaubert had bypassed questions of morality or anodyne consolation to ask himself a single question: Is that true? But Sainte-Beuve found that the ideal was too much absent and asserted, "Moreover, if truth alone is sought, it is not entirely and necessarily to be found only on the side of evil, on the side of human stupidity and perversity." He concluded, in spite of his reservations, that "in every respect the book carries the signature of the times in which it has appeared." This judgment, and the accompanying reservations, are not inapplicable to Flaubert's American successor.

A final word about John Dos Passos the man. We have seen that in his novels he is by design self-effac-

ing except for the revelations of sensibility in the
Camera Eyes. Even when he writes with passionate
concern for those who perpetually get a raw deal there
is a clinical detachment which largely depersonalizes
him. But we do get to see another side of him. He
reveals himself as the warm, enthusiastic, intellectually
curious fellow he was in *Chosen Country*, where the
reader takes pleasure in linking him with Jay Pignatelli.
The Best Times conveys his spirit of youthful adventure in an engaging way. Even though it carries him
only up to his marriage with Katharine Smith and the
beginning of the depression and even though it is wise
to bear in mind that this autobiography is retrospec-
tive—forty years later—still it gives a warming sense
of the zestful, perennially questing young man, full of
energy and open of mind and spirit. Best of all are the
recently published letters and diary fragments in *The
Fourteenth Chronicle* (1973). They span his entire
life. They show him as warm and faithful in friendship, as a passionate seeker of truth, as an often re-
laxed observer of life, as one capable of laughing at
himself and others, above all as a modest, honest, and
lovable man.

Bibliography

1. Books by John Dos Passos

One Man's Initiation—1917. London: Allen & Unwin, 1920. Reprinted as *First Encounter.* New York: Philosophical Library, 1945; and as *One Man's Initiation: 1917.* Ithaca, N.Y.: Cornell University Press, 1969.

Three Soldiers. New York: George H. Doran Company, 1921.

A Pushcart at the Curb. New York: George H. Doran Company, 1922.

Rosinante to the Road Again. New York: George H. Doran Company, 1922.

Streets of Night. New York: George H. Doran Company, 1923.

Manhattan Transfer. Boston: Houghton Mifflin Company, 1925.

Facing the Chair: Story of the Americanization of Two Foreignborn Workmen. Boston: Sacco-Vanzetti Defense Committee, 1927. Reprinted by New York: Da Capo Press, 1970.

Orient Express. New York: Harper & Brothers, 1927.

The 42nd Parallel. Boston: Houghton Mifflin Company, 1930.

1919. Boston: Houghton Mifflin Company, 1932.

Three Plays. New York: Harcourt, Brace & Company, 1934.

In All Countries. New York: Harcourt, Brace & Company, 1934.

The Big Money. Boston: Houghton Mifflin Company, 1936.

U.S.A. New York: Modern Library, 1937–38.

The Villages Are the Heart of Spain. New York: Esquire-Coronet, 1937.

Journeys Between Wars. New York: Harcourt, Brace & Company, 1938.

Adventures of a Young Man. Boston: Houghton Mifflin Company, 1939.

The Living Thoughts of Tom Paine. New York: Longmans, Green, 1940.

The Ground We Stand On: Some Examples from the History of a Political Creed. New York: Harcourt, Brace & Company, 1941.

Number One. Boston: Houghton Mifflin Company, 1943.

State of the Nation. Boston: Houghton Mifflin Company, 1944.

Tour of Duty. Boston: Houghton Mifflin Company, 1946.

The Grand Design. Boston: Houghton Mifflin Company, 1949.

The Prospect Before Us. Boston: Houghton Mifflin Company, 1950.

Chosen Country. Boston: Houghton Mifflin Company, 1951.

District of Columbia. Boston: Houghton Mifflin Company, 1952.

The Head and Heart of Thomas Jefferson. Garden City, N.Y.: Doubleday & Company, 1954.

Most Likely to Succeed. Englewood Cliffs, N.J.: Prentice-Hall, Inc., 1954.

The Theme Is Freedom. New York: Dodd, Mead & Company, 1956.

The Men Who Made the Nation. Garden City, N.Y.: Doubleday & Company, 1957.

The Great Days. New York: Sagamore Press, 1958.

Prospects of a Golden Age. Englewood Cliffs, N.J.: Prentice-Hall, Inc., 1959.

Midcentury. Boston: Houghton Mifflin Company, 1961.

Mr. Wilson's War. Garden City, N.Y.: Doubleday & Company, 1962.

Brazil on the Move. Garden City, N.Y.: Doubleday & Company, 1963.

Occasions and Protests. Chicago: Henry Regnery Co., 1964.

The Shackles of Power. Garden City, N.Y.: Doubleday & Company, 1966.

The Best Times: An Informal Memoir. New York: New American Library, 1966.

The Portugal Story: Three Centuries of Exploration and Discovery. Garden City, N.Y.: Doubleday & Company, 1969.

Easter Island: Island of Enigmas. Garden City, N.Y.: Doubleday & Company, 1971.

Century's Ebb. Boston: Gambit Inc., 1974.

2. Books about John Dos Passos

Astre, Georges Albert. *Thèmes et Structures dans l'oeuvre de John Dos Passos.* Paris: Lettres Modernes, 1958.

Belkind, Allen, ed. *Dos Passos, the Critics, and the Writer's Intention.* Carbondale: Southern Illinois University Press, 1971.

Brantley, John D. *The Fiction of John Dos Passos.* The Hague: Mouton, 1968.

Knox, George A., and Stahl, Herbert M. *Dos Passos and "The Revolting Playwrights."* Uppsala: Uppsala University Press, 1964.

Landsberg, Melvin. *Dos Passos' Path to U.S.A.: A Political Biography 1912–1936.* Boulder: Colorado Associated University Press, 1972.

Ludington, Townsend, ed. *The Fourteenth Chronicle: Letters and Diaries of John Dos Passos.* Boston: Gambit Inc., 1973.

Sanders, David, ed. *Studies in U.S.A.* Columbus, O.: Charles E. Merrill Publishing Company, 1972.

Wrenn, John H. *John Dos Passos.* New York: Twayne Publishers, 1961.

3. Other Critical Writings

Aaron, Daniel. "The Adventures of John Dos Passos." In *Writers on the Left*, pp. 343–53. New York: Harcourt, Brace & Company, 1961.

———. "The Riddle of Dos Passos." *Harpers* 224 (March 1962):55–60.

Aldridge, John W. "Dos Passos: The Energy of Despair." In *After the Lost Generation*, pp. 59–81. New York: McGraw Hill, 1951.

Beach, Joseph Warren. "Dos Passos: 1947." *Sewanee Review* 55 (Summer 1947):406–18.

Bernardin, Charles W. "Dos Passos' Harvard Years." *New England Quarterly* 27 (March 1954):23–26.

Chametzky, Jules. "Reflections on *U.S.A.* as Novel and Play." *Massachusetts Review* 1 (February 1960):391–99.

Cowley, Malcolm. "Dos Passos and His Critics." *New Republic* 120 (February 28, 1949):21–23.

Davis, Robert Gorham. *John Dos Passos* (Pamphlet). Minneapolis: University of Minnesota Press, 1962.

Frohock, W. M. "John Dos Passos: Of Time and Frustration." *Southwest Review* 33 (1948):71–80. See also *The Novel of Violence in America*, pp. 23–51. Dallas: Southern Methodist University Press, 1957.

Geismar, Maxwell. "John Dos Passos: Conversion of a Hero." In *Writers in Crisis*, pp. 87–139. Boston: Houghton Mifflin Company, 1942.

Gelfant, Blanche H. "The Search for Identity in the Novels of John Dos Passos." *PMLA* 76 (March 1961):133–49.

Kallich, Martin. "John Dos Passos Fellow-Traveler: A Dossier with Commentary." *Twentieth Century Literature* 1 (January 1956): 173–90.

———. "John Dos Passos: Liberty and the Father Image." *Antioch Review* 10 (March 1950):100–105.

Kazin, Alfred. "John Dos Passos: Inventor in Isolation." *Saturday Review*, March 15, 1969, pp. 16–19, 44–45.

Knox, George A. "Dos Passos and Painting." *Texas Studies in Literature and Language* 6 (1964):22–38.

Leavis, F. R. "A Serious Artist." *Scrutiny* 1 (September 1932):173–79.

Sanders, David. "The 'Anarchism' of John Dos Passos." *South Atlantic Quarterly* 60 (Winter 1961):44–45.

———. " 'Lies' and the System: Enduring Themes from Dos Passos' Early Novels." *South Atlantic Quarterly* 65 (Summer 1966):215–28.

Sartre, Jean-Paul. "A Propos de John Dos Passos et de '1919.' " In *Situations I*, pp. 14–25. Paris: Gallimard, 1947. See also *Literary Essays*, pp. 88–96. New York: Philosophical Library, 1957.

Schwartz, Delmore. "John Dos Passos and the Whole Truth." *Southern Review* 4 (October 1938):351–67.

Smith, James S. "The Novelist of Discomfort: A Reconsideration of John Dos Passos." *College English* 19 (May 1958):332–38.

Stoltzfus, Ben. "John Dos Passos and the French." *Comparative Literature* 15 (Spring 1963):146–63.

Trilling, Lionel. "The America of John Dos Passos." *Partisan Review* 4 (April 1938):26–32.

Index